WHITEFIELD PUBLIC LIBRARY
WHITEFIELD, N. H. 03598

J 796.33
K

DISCARDED

BOOKS BY DON KOWET

Pelé   1975
Vida Blue: Coming Up Again   1974
Golden Toes: Football's Greatest Kickers   1972

PELÉ

PELÉ

Don Kowet

ATHENEUM / SMI   NEW YORK   **1976**

Library of Congress Cataloging in Publication Data
Kowet, Don. Pelé.
1. Nascimento, Edson Arantes do, 1940-
2. Soccer. I. Title GV942.7.N3K68
796.33'4'0924 (B) ISBN 0-689-10713-7
75-38344

Copyright © 1976 by Don Kowet
All rights reserved
Manufactured in the United States of America
Composition by Dix Typesetting Co. Inc., Syracuse, New York
Printed by Carney Printing Co., Nashville, Tennessee
Bound by The Nicholstone Book Bindery, Inc.,
Nashville, Tennessee
Designed by Kathleen Carey
First Edition

TO BEGOÑA

*Without her help,
I'd still be teaching English
in Algorta.*

Contents

1	Spreading the News	3
2	Preaching—and Practicing	15
3	The Return of Pelé	27
4	The Greening of Pelé	37
5	A Rival—and a Riot	52
6	The King of England, the Queen of Hearts	72
7	What Makes Pelé Pelé?	83
8	Clive Toye's 75,000-Mile Odyssey: The Signing of Pelé	92
9	The Selling of Pelé	107
10	Planting the Seed	119

Illustrations

An album of photographs follows page 63.

ALL PHOTOGRAPHS REPRODUCED BY COURTESY OF UNITED PRESS INTERNATIONAL.

PELÉ

1

Spreading the News

AT TWO O'CLOCK in the afternoon of June 11, 1975, a crowd of curious onlookers overflowed the sidewalk and caused a traffic jam outside Manhattan's posh 21 Club. Car drivers blew their horns; cabbies and truckers simply blew their cool, craning their necks out the windows of their cabs to bellow obscenities. A traffic cop who swaggered up from the intersection of Fifty-second Street and Fifth Avenue had no more luck turning back that human tide than the Pharaoh, in hot pursuit of Moses, had rolling back the Red Sea.

The chaos outside of the 21 Club was only exceeded by the consternation within. In a room built to accom-

CHAPTER ONE

modate 100 diners, 300 headline-hungry agents of the world's sporting press were packed armpit to elbow. "Gentlemen of the press," pleaded Clive Toye, general manager of the New York Cosmos soccer team, "will you *please* behave yourselves!" All around him, eyeglasses were being knocked off noses and onto the floor, there to be trampled by "gentlemen of the press" who were jostling for position with elbows as lethal as muggers' knives.

Compounding the confusion, suicide squads of gatecrashers—mostly female, almost all young and pretty—had charmed their way past the credentials desk. Throughout the press conference their exotic squeals added a grating soprano to the queries, the complaints, and the propaganda.

"He's so *short*," giggled a pretty young thing, stretching on tiptoes.

There, in the eye of the storm, stood the cause of all this uncommon commotion: A small (5 feet, 8 inches), solidly constructed black man, in a black brocaded silk leisure suit, a button proclaiming the slogan "Big Apple" in red pinned to one lapel.

"I want to *touch* him," moaned her girl friend. "Not because he's a sex symbol," she added quickly, "but because he's just the best athlete in the *world*."

Henry Aaron was never invited to Buckingham Palace by the Queen of England; Arnold Palmer was never awarded the French Legion of Honor; Muhammad Ali was never the cause of a truce in a civil war; and it's not likely that Joe Namath will ever obtain an audience with the Pope. Only one man had done all these things, and more: Pelé—a synonym for superstar on five continents, richer than any other athlete, and with more disciples than the most compelling avatar.

If you mentioned "El Rey" to teen-agers dribbling a soccer ball in the plaza of some desperate Spanish backwater, they'd know you meant the current King of Soccer, not the new King of Spain. When "El Peligro" ("The Danger") came to Santiago, Chileans ran toward their football stadium, not their earthquake shelters. In France, he was "La Tulipe Noire"; in Portugal he was "La Perola Negra"—anywhere that soccer was played (and that was almost everywhere) the name Pelé kindled a special awe. He was as Brazilian as coffee, as French as a liver ailment, as Spanish as a civil war. And finally, on June 11, 1975, he was about to become as American as pizza and Stravinsky and the compact car.

"Gentlemen, *gentlemen*, we don't want anybody to get *killed* here," Clive Toye had to shout, his carefully groomed white hair wilting in the suffocating heat, worry lines furrowing the forehead of a face round as the soccer ball between Pelé's hands. "Please," Toye said, "let's have some *order*."

But the story was too big, the moment too pregnant. Once an Italian team called Juventus had offered Pelé a $300,000 bonus to sign a contract; he turned them down cold. Once a Spanish team called Real Madrid had tried to tempt him with a blank check, endorsed by the club's directors; Pelé sent it back by return mail. And only a few years back, three leading Italian teams had pooled their resources and offered Santos, Pelé's Brazilian club, $2 million to part with their superstar. Brazil's President then, Janio Quadros, had acted swiftly in this "national crisis." He had designated Pelé an official "national treasure," making him, as if he were some portrait painted by a venerated master, unexportable.

Yet, the day before, on June 10, in Bermuda, the greatest soccer player who had ever lived had signed the first part of the greatest sports contract ever awarded. Over the next three years, his combined promotional contract with Warner Communications, Inc., and his player's contract with the New York Cosmos of the North American Soccer League (NASL) would be worth to him at least $4.5 million. It didn't matter that a vast majority of Americans still thought, as Clive Toye once put it, "that any guy who runs around in short pants kicking a ball is either a communist or a fairy." It didn't matter that Pelé was thirty-four years old and was making a comeback after an eight-month retirement. It didn't matter that the star of so many Brazilian World Cup teams would have the word "Cosmos" emblazoned across his chest, playing out the twilight days of his fabulous career in the eternal twilight of Downing Stadium, on Randall's Island, beneath the Triborough Bridge.

Pelé—ending his premature abdication, transformed from king into troll, nudging short precise passes toward teammates whose names were as forgettable as his was renowned.

Bulbs popped. Hot TV lights simmered. On a dais up front, Pelé posed patiently, a soccer ball in his right hand, a metal New York Cosmos emblem hanging on the wall behind his left shoulder, the expression on his broad, handsome face modulating from bewilderment to amusement, as the uproar swelled. His wife, Rosemarie, stood in a far corner, nervously puffing a cigarette. She smiled shyly for the cameras, then with more warmth, as her husband flashed a "V"-for-victory sign at her. At the bidding of some photographers, she went and kissed her husband.

"Oh," a pretty young gate-crasher (the one who had vowed she had come to see the world's best athlete, not its biggest sex symbol) said glumly. "That must be his wife."

And then came the barrage of questions, the verbal tiger-traps laid by reporters who wanted to know why the Cosmos had been willing to spend such a staggering sum; why Pelé felt compelled to accept; whether he could, at thirty-four, still perform those airy flights of soccer magic.

Speaking mostly in Portuguese, through an interpreter, Pelé proved he was as clever on the dais as he was on the soccer field. He dribbled past barbed questions (How did he rate American soccer?) and deftly set up general manager Toye with opportunities to score effective public relations points. He sprinkled his answers with potent wisecracks that disarmed his interrogators and made them laugh.

And then he grew serious.

"Everyone in life has a mission," he said soberly, "and my dream is that one day the United States will know soccer like the rest of the world. This is the only country in which soccer was not a major sport, and I had a dream that one day the sport would come here with my help."

He was being sincere—but he was being diplomatic. He could have said more. He might have pointed out that, measured on a global scale, American athletes were strictly minor-league. That from Terry Bradshaw and O. J. Simpson to Vida Blue and Reggie Jackson, from Kareem Abdul-Jabbar and Walt Frazier to Bobby Orr and Bernie Parent, the U.S. pros were world-wide nobodies. They might be strong, they might be swift and they might be wealthy, but they all suffered from the same international flaw: None of them played the supreme sport, soccer.

The previous January, American networks, newspapers and magazines boasted that 80 million people, in person or in front of TV sets, had watched the National Football League Super Bowl. But only a few months before, when West Germany won soccer's most recent World Cup competition, it was seen by *900 million* people on five continents.

Pelé knew that Americans take great, if envious, pride in the vast salaries paid to the top pros—the handful who earn in excess of $100,000 a year. Yet he also knew that when Brazil won the World Cup in 1970—led, of course, in fact and in spirit by Pelé—every member of the squad earned a minimum of $103,000 *in addition* to his regular salary. Even then Pelé was a human conglomerate who probably could have afforded Joe Namath as a subsidiary.

Pelé could have said all these things, but instead opted for a somewhat more subtle approach.

"For the first time in Brazil's history," he said, "we are exporting know-how to you, instead of importing it."

If his arrival in this country had aroused the hysteria sparked by the Beatles, the conviction behind his words evoked in his listeners the reverence habitually reserved for popes. Even the most skeptical were won over by his refreshing bluntness about his own enormous talents.

"Today, soccer has arrived in the United States," he concluded, without a trace of false modesty. "Spread the news."

Then, proving himself a savvy trouper, as the press conference drew to a close, he made sure he left his audience laughing. "I have just one small problem," he confided, as the reporters were pushing the caps onto their ballpoint pens, stuffing tape recorders into their attaché cases. A problem? The press paused, leaning forward in anticipation. "When I signed the contract," Pelé continued, his broad mouth breaking into a grin, "they didn't tell me I had to try out. But now the coach says I have to make the team."

CHAPTER ONE

Everyone laughed.

No one stopped to wonder if the joke contained a kernel of self-doubt.

After all, Pelé was venturing north at age thirty-four, a self-styled missionary whose self-appointed task was to teach Americans to think with their feet, to convert them to the catechism of crossed balls and headers. It was a remarkable act, a courageous one for a man already worth some $10 million, who could have eased into legend without ever again submitting his skills to public scrutiny. The Warner Corporation, owners of the Cosmos, were only wagering $4.5 million. Edson Arantes do Nascimento was risking the priceless prestige evoked by the nickname "Pelé."

But already Pelé had produced an early, and unanticipated, dividend. Last night, Bob Wussler, vice-president of CBS sports, had confirmed that Pelé's first game the following Sunday, an exhibition against the Dallas Tornado at Downing Stadium, would be televised nationally, with the Cosmos receiving $50,000—half from CBS, and the other half from a company called Global TV, which intended to broadcast the game both to Pelé's native Brazil and to Venezuela. For years the NASL had been trying to entice a major network into transmitting its games nationwide. Without national television exposure—and eventually a network contract—NASL commissioner Phil Woosnam knew that no major sports promotion could succeed. Asked about plans for additional soccer coverage on

CBS, Wussler said, "A lot depends on Sunday's ratings."

If Pelé's ability to obtain national TV exposure was crucial to the future of the league, his ability to lure paying customers through the turnstiles, at home and on the road, was crucial to the Cosmos, if they were ever to recover the enormous sum they had invested in him. A source close to the Cosmos revealed that the club would receive 50 percent of the gross gate above the pre-Pelé average at all away games.

Sunday's exhibition match against the Tornado would provide an early clue to whether that $4.5 million gamble was destined to pay off.

Meanwhile, a telephone call to the Cosmos' head office during the press conference turned up an interesting bit of irony. The Cosmos had left one very lonesome temporary employee in their offices to handle hundreds of calls. "I'm *trying* to be nice," the girl said. But, she admitted, after a while it got depressing, having to explain about the press conference called to publicize Pelé and his $4.5 million contract, for $2.50 an hour.

That evening, in Philadelphia, Pelé made his debut as a Cosmo. Not as a player, but as a personality. The Cosmos were scheduled to play the Philadelphia Atoms, and even in civilian clothes, the superstar from Brazil completely dominated the stadium. As soon as he emerged from the visitors' dugout—a sleek, dark

CHAPTER ONE

figure, his coffee-colored skin in striking contrast to his white leather jacket—most of the 20,124 fans (about 10,000 above average) began chanting, "We want Pelé, We want Pelé," the litany swelling in volume as he strolled slowly toward midfield.

It was a poignant moment. By the time Pelé reached the center of the field, all of the spectators were on their feet, applauding and cheering, paying homage to a man whom most had never even seen play. In the executive box high atop the stadium, Pelé's wife, Rosie, was watching, too—until tears blurred her eyes. And then the poignant moment gave way to a historic one, as Pelé executed not the most accurate kick of his career, nor even the cleverest, but surely the most significant. He kicked the soccer ball lightly with his right foot. It rolled five yards—nearly one yard for every million the Cosmos were paying him to bring soccer to this last isolated outpost.

As soon as he stepped onto the field, it became obvious he could inspire American fans. As soon as the game started, it became just as obvious it would take his performance as well as his presence to inspire his Cosmos teammates to play winning soccer. For the two halves (forty-five minutes each) of regulation time, the Atoms attacked relentlessly, and only the supple acrobatics of Cosmos goalie Sam Nusam prevented a score. The Cosmos lacked coordination. Their passes were erratic, each pass followed by an interception. Soon the Cosmos had abandoned the vital midfield area to huddle miserably around their goal in a last-ditch defense. Then, five minutes into the fifteen-minute sudden-death overtime, their luck ran out. Trying to clear the ball from in front of his own goal, the Cosmos' Luis de la Fuente passed the ball straight to Philadelphia's John McLaughlin. McLaughlin laid the ball off to Chris Bahr, and Bahr drove an 18-yarder, low and hard, into the Cosmos' nets. The Atoms had won a well-earned, 1–0 victory.

Before the game, Pelé had been in a jovial mood; when someone suggested that the reason he didn't dress for the game was that the Cosmos didn't have enough money left to get his uniform out of the cleaners, he had laughed harder than anyone. After the game, however, his mood had altered. He was somber. He had seen the Cosmos play and had been appalled. Throughout his eighteen-year career, he had maintained a firm rule never to criticize his teammates. Now he observed that rule, yet bent it ever so slightly. He refused to single out individual Cosmos for criticism, but his assessment of the team's overall play was as scathing as it was precise. It was clear he was criticizing not to embarrass, but to instruct.

"As was the case with the Vancouver game which I saw two weeks ago," said Pelé, "I found that the Cosmos have a number of good players, but their style is too individual. I thought the Cosmos' defenders played well, but their forwards were too slow," he added. "They were disorganized on the field and they didn't play well together as a team. I feel," he concluded, "from what I have seen, here the game is more of a running game, where in Brazil it is more technical. But that doesn't mean you can't use the technique that you have," he emphasized.

The message was clear. It wouldn't be enough to play *with* Pelé. You had to play *like* Pelé.

That following week, Pelé gave some of his less adept teammates an education not only in the finesse of soccer, but in its fundamentals.

2

Preaching—and Practicing

It was a hectic week for Pelé, full of interviews and personal appearances that brought the Cosmos—until then virtually ignored by the New York press—ounces of free ink in publicity. The newsmen who toiled for the New York dailies—traditionally ornery, skeptical, and querulous—were both mystified and enchanted by the Brazilian, so accustomed had they become to the self-indulgent narcissism of a Muhammad Ali, or the playboy picaresque of a Joe Namath.

Although Pelé had a higher value in the flesh market than Namath, reporters noted, still he could sit in a private box throughout that game in Philadelphia, shyly holding hands with his wife.

CHAPTER TWO

Pelé had Ali's quick wit, Ali's candid appraisal of himself as "the greatest," yet where Ali seemed to be bragging, Pelé could pat himself on the back and still seem humble. When Pelé said, "My talent is the gift of God—I am only what he made me," there was a conviction in his voice that the moody, volatile, erratic, yet brilliant Ali could never convey.

And something else impressed the American journalists, grown accustomed to the arrogance of athletes whose bodies have been pampered and protected by recruiters and coaches, sought after by hordes of hungry groupies, till they are convinced that because they are more "tele-visible" than ordinary men, they are better than ordinary men. Pelé was unfailingly polite. No matter how repetitious or infuriating or idiotic the question, he always responded with a smile—and acted with the common touch. Posing one day for photographers in Manhattan's Central Park, for example, he was suddenly surrounded by scores of youngsters—mostly blacks and Puerto Ricans. Pelé turned his back on the photographers. He passed up the chance to have his picture taken encircled by kids—a favorite pose for American superstars, who, more likely than not, will then refuse to give autographs the moment the last flash bulb has popped. Instead, he implored those teenagers to "play the game often"; he reminded them that none of them had ever known more poverty than Edson Arantes do Nascimento, whom the world calls Pelé.

PREACHING—AND PRACTICING

The meteoric rise of Edson Arantes do Nascimento began in a small town in the Brazilian interior called Três Corações (Three Hearts). Pelé's father, João Ramos do Nascimento, was a part-time journeyman soccer player with the nickname Dondhino. (Every Brazilian player is known by a nickname, some of which are meaningful, others obscure. Pelé himself has no idea how he got his nickname, or its significance.) When Pelé was five, Dondhino was promoted to a slightly higher-class team in Bauru and moved there with his wife, Celeste, and their three children. To supplement his meager income as a soccer player, Dondhino became a minor clerk in the civil service. Seven people were packed into the family's tiny, two-bedroom house. Pelé's main playground was the streets.

Soon Pelé had a reputation in the neighborhood as a genius at soccer—and something less at his studies. His grades in school were poor, and he left after the fourth grade, by mutual agreement with a truant officer whose stern face he still remembers clearly. From then on, Pelé devoted all his energies toward one goal: perfecting his soccer skills.

There was, however, one problem. Dondhino couldn't even afford to buy his son a soccer ball. So, as black basketball players born into rural poverty in the South will do, Pelé stuffed a sock with rags, and kicked that. Then he discovered he could get even better results using a grapefruit. By the time he was ten, however, he was determined to own a real

CHAPTER TWO

ball. So he sold peanuts in front of local movie houses and shined shoes until he had saved enough cash.

"Football was the only career I ever thought of," he says. "I became a cobbler's apprentice (earning two dollars a month), but I never really thought I'd stick to it. I wanted to follow my father's path. I was convinced he was the best player who ever lived, but that he never got the chance to prove it."

Pelé got his chance from a former São Paulo player named Waldemar de Brito. The year was 1952, and de Brito—who lived in Bauru—was watching a group of construction workers in a pickup soccer game. "Of all the players in that game," de Brito recalled later, "only one stood out. I immediately spotted what could only be called genius."

De Brito took that scrawny eleven-year-old—whose shabby clothes contrasted with his polished skills—under his wing. Tall and slim, with a gruff manner and a deep, rumbling voice, de Brito intimidated Pelé into training long, hard hours. Four years de Brito spent honing Pelé's natural abilities, so that by the time he was fourteen, Pelé was playing for the same Bauru team as his father. The following year, with the blessings of Dondhino and Celeste, de Brito bought Pelé his first pair of long trousers. Then, like Dick Whittington's cat, the pair went off to seek their fortune in the coastal city of São Paulo.

But the big-headed big-leaguers of São Paulo were unimpressed by a reputation earned in a minor-league backwater like Bauru. "I was very naive," says Pelé, "but I really thought I could make some team." Pelé was mistaken. The city-slick coaches he performed for were less naive than he, but they were—to their eternal embarrassment—even more wrong. They turned Pelé down, so the determined de Brito led his disappointed protégé to the seacoast city of Santos. There he presented the awed fifteen-year-old to the coach of the Santos club, Luiz Alonso Perez, with the astonishing introduction: "This boy will be the greatest soccer player in the world!"

Perez, known as "Lula," agreed to look at Pelé. Thrown into a practice session with veteran pros, Pelé quickly demonstrated de Brito's confidence in him to be well founded, relying on his cleverness and speed to beat older, bigger players. After that one session, and an argument with reluctant club officials, Lula hired Pelé on a trial basis. His pay was a meager six thousand cruzeiros a month—seventy-five dollars.

Pelé's self-confidence, severely weakened by his rejection in São Paulo, was slow to return to him in Santos. "I felt as if I was lost," he recalls. "I was only fifteen and suddenly I had to live with strange people in a strange place. I was scared of failing, but even more I was scared of the dark." After two months, he was still a little afraid of the dark dormitory where the team lived, and of the city—so large, impersonal, and uncaring. But it was becoming apparent that, despite his fears, he was not going to fail on the field. In 1956, he graduated from the junior team to the reserves of the Santos first team, with a salary hike to about six

CHAPTER TWO

hundred dollars a month. When, in his first game for Santos, the team won, 7–1, with Pelé scoring four of the seven goals, club officials finally lost their skepticism. Proof that they now had confidence in Pelé's future, they gave a bonus of one thousand dollars to de Brito, who returned home to Bauru, his place in the legend of Pelé secure.

Lula was another who would loom large in that legend. Soft-spoken, unflappable, Lula was an astute strategist, a clever manipulator of men, but he would always be known simply as the man who coached Pelé. Not that Lula objected to playing second-fiddle. "Pelé," he was fond of repeating, with appropriate pauses for dramatic effect, "is not only the greatest player I ever coached. He is the greatest player *anyone* ever coached."

So, years later, in Central Park, when Pelé assured those star-struck black and Puerto Rican kids that with God's divine help, and their own mortal sweat, they too could scale the pinnacles of fame and wealth, he was merely preaching what he had practiced.

But Pelé could only sustain the common touch so far. While his new teammates, many of whom still held day jobs as draftsmen and clerical workers and plumbers, were commuting between home and practice field in vehicles as unglamorous as city buses, Pelé was arriving by limousine from his plush suite in a mid-Manhattan hotel. Beside him, likewise in air-conditioned comfort, sat his most intimate friend and per-

PREACHING—AND PRACTICING

sonal adviser, Julio Mazzei, whom the Cosmos had also hired. Mazzei had been the trainer for Santos, Pelé's club in Brazil until he retired in October 1974.

"With the Cosmos, Mazzei will continue to run clinics with Pelé, in conjunction with the Pepsi-Cola program, and will assist coach Gordon Bradley in the preparation of the team," general manager Clive Toye had explained at the signing ceremony. Pelé called Mazzei "Professor" and "Daddy," leaving no doubt about the depth of their relationship and their mutual regard. Still, some observers wondered whether in signing Mazzei, the Cosmos had sown the seeds of a potential conflict. Would Pelé have one coach while his teammates had another?

Pelé's first workout with the Cosmos was held during a rainstorm inside the gym at Long Island's Hofstra University. His chauffeur had gotten lost in the maze of intersecting highways out from Manhattan, and Pelé arrived 38 minutes late.

Pelé, of course, has always made an obsession of being prompt. Once, for the shooting of an instructional film produced by Pepsi-Cola (which pays him $200,000 annually to do promotional work), he was warned not to be "late like everyone else in Brazil." The shooting was to begin at 8 A.M. At 7:45, a friend saw Pelé drive one of his Volkswagens a half block from the stadium and stop. Pelé sat in the car for ten minutes. Then he got out and walked slowly to the field. At exactly 8:00 he walked onto the field—smiling.

CHAPTER TWO

This day, his first practice with the Cosmos, he apologized to Cosmos coach Gordon Bradley, who waived the customary twenty-five-dollar fine for tardiness. Then Pelé addressed his new teammates: "I've always been a team man, and I still am," he said. "Please don't expect me to win games alone. We must work together."

Then he went to one side of the basketball court and, under the watchful eye of Julio Mazzei, performed a rugged program of calisthenics. When he and Mazzei decided his muscles were supple enough, Pelé participated in the first of two successive six-aside soccer games. His presence as the newest—and best—player on the team had an immediate impact.

The first to feel it was Alfredo Lamas, up to then considered the Cosmos' top dribbler. Each time Lamas attempted to dribble past Pelé, the Brazilian deftly hooked the ball away from his feet. It was as if the Knicks' Walt Frazier had somehow showed up for a high school basketball game, stealing the ball from anyone who dared penetrate his defensive perimeter.

Then Pelé demonstrated another facet of his complex soccer personality. The incident occurred late in the training session, when Pelé took a pass at half-court, beat two defenders, and found himself face to face with starting goalkeeper Sam Nusam. Pelé looked at Sam. The lanky, black Bermudan looked back at Pelé—poised there, with the ball on his foot, a foot capable of delivering one of the most powerful shots the game has ever known. For Nusam, frozen before

PREACHING—AND PRACTICING

that living legend, completely at Pelé's mercy, it was a moment that seemed almost eternal. In all the world, there was just him—and that foot able to kick a soccer ball with the force of a sledge hammer. Then, astonishingly, Pelé smiled. He didn't shoot. He flicked the ball back to a teammate.

"I think," said the grateful Nusam, "that if he had taken that shot, the Cosmos might be in the market for a new goalie. He could have torn my head off."

Afterwards, Pelé jogged almost two miles, then finished off with another set of exercises. "Most of those exercises are to build up the abdominal muscles, which are the most important to soccer players," explained Mazzei.

When asked to assess Pelé's current physical condition, given the fact that since his retirement almost nine months before, Pelé had played in only six matches, all exhibitions, Mazzei replied, "I would say that he's now seventy percent physically perfect, and should be one hundred percent in about ten days." Mazzei then added that, whatever his immediate physical limitations, Pelé intended to lead the Cosmos against Dallas the following Sunday like a field marshal. "He'll be yelling out instructions, in what language I don't know," Mazzei promised, "to get his teammates moving in a well-organized formation. From what I have seen," he added, "that is the biggest problem of the team. It resembles the United Nations—a lot of different styles."

As was becoming his trademark, Pelé ended that first practice session on a humorous note. When a

CHAPTER TWO

woman reporter from Argentina asked him if he was ready to answer some questions, he replied: "Of course, as long as your questions don't deal with cooking. Those you will have to ask my wife."

On Friday, the Cosmos practiced again, this time at Downing Stadium, and this time Pelé arrived on time. A few days before, in answer to a reporter's question, Pelé had singled out two Cosmos players for special praise by their numbers, since he didn't know their names. Apparently embarrassed by that episode, from the start that day he began calling to teammates by name, meanwhile applauding every good move each of them made.

There were, of course, cynics who had predicted that Pelé—with his high salary, his fame, his knack for drawing the spotlight—would be resented by the players he overshadowed. After all, some of them were earning only a few thousand dollars per season, while The King was commanding a suitable ransom. But instead of resenting him, the Cosmos idolized him. Approaching his new teammate, Gil Mardarescu, a midfielder from Rumania, said, "I dreamed of some day just shaking your hand. But to *play* with you, this is a miracle!" Then he made the sign of the cross.

Toward the end of that morning session, in an intrasquad game observed by a large contingent of photographers and reporters, Pelé produced another kind of miracle, proving that although his skills might still need polishing after the long layoff, no rust had set in.

PREACHING—AND PRACTICING

Standing with his back to the opponents' goal, Pelé took a sharply angled, waist-high pass from midfielder Johnny Kerr, bicycled himself into the air, and blasted an overhead kick past second-string goalkeeper Kurt Kuykendall. The spectators and players on both sides all applauded furiously, all except goalie Kuykendall.

"What happened?" he asked.

After practice, Pelé jogged for several miles, Mazzei watching him like a fussy show-biz momma witnessing her prodigy's pro acting debut. He followed his run with a set of calisthenics, and, after showering and dressing, slipped quietly away in his black limousine toward Purchase, New York, in Westchester County, home of Pepsi-Cola's suburban headquarters.

In a pastoral setting, where secretaries sunbathe among Alexander Calder and Henry Moore sculptures, Pelé met Don Kendall, chairman of the board of PepsiCo. Kendall told Pelé: "Mia casa es sua casa" ("My house is your house").

Pelé took one glance at Kendall's seven-building complex, and replied, in English, with a grin: "Are you sure?"

For two hours, Pelé worked out in PepsiCo's lavishly equipped gymnasium; then, the long ride back to Manhattan. As the black limo sped onwards, it became clear that amid all the fanfare given his $4.5 million contract, and his messianic zeal toward promoting soccer, one deep-rooted motive for coming to play here had been overlooked. More than the works of famous sculptors or the clusters of pretty secretaries

CHAPTER TWO

surrounding them, what had most impressed Pelé that afternoon, and given him an afternoon of bliss, was the PepsiCo headquarters' utter isolation.

"Everybody needs a moment by himself," Pelé murmured, peering as he spoke at the traffic rushing toward the city. "It's impossible for me to get that in England or Germany, but maybe it will be different here."

"Then you don't really want to make the United States as soccer-crazy as the rest of the world?" someone asked him.

"Of course I do," he replied softly. "But the United States has lots of famous people in movies and sports. Here I will be just one of many stars."

And then he recalled how the notion had dawned on him that the United States might be the last haven left, his final chance to live a normal life: A few years earlier, as he and Rosie were strolling along Los Angeles' Hollywood Boulevard, he suddenly realized that the passers-by were completely unaware of him. He realized that he was not being mobbed by fans nor smothered by security guards nor pestered by reporters nor tugged at by autograph hounds. . . . And then he stopped. He did something he had dreamed of doing for years. In the midst of that uncaring crowd of shoppers, Pelé hoisted his astonished wife into the air.

"I'm free," he shouted. "I'm *free!*"

3

The Return of Pelé

THE GUARDS AT DINGY, dimly lit Downing Stadium had never seen a Sunday like this one. A full house, almost twenty-two thousand—five thousand more than Clive Toye's pregame estimate, and more than double the Cosmos' previous best.

The guards at Downing Stadium had never seen so many people, nor so many *famous* people. Throughout the week, celebrities, or their secretaries, had been badgering the Cosmos' publicist, John O'Reilly, with ticket requests. Now, before the startled eyes of the wizened old-timers in baggy cop clothes, the blue bloods of New York's show-biz and media cliques were meeting and greeting, laughing the way they did

CHAPTER THREE

when they went slumming on Saturday nights to McDonald's—not just the man from the Six O'Clock News, not just the lady whose face evoked images from some long-ago movie, but authentic celebrities, too: Mayor Abe Beame, for instance, taking time out from trying to transform the stony silence of New York bankers into gold, to watch the debut of Pelé; and *Robert Redford was there,* the reigning celluloid king come to pay homage to the king of soccer.

The guards at the stadium blinked. They rubbed their eyes and strained their ears. My God, almost twenty-two thousand people, *and almost every one of them spoke English!*

Not down on the field, though, where three hundred newsmen from all over the world were concocting a multilingual stew, soft Brazilian sounds getting impaled on German syllables, Spanish competing with Russian, Italian clashing with English—the whole unintelligible babel pressing toward some instant Esperanto. Along the sidelines, 150 cameramen were jostling for position with the ferocity of housewives at a one-dollar clearance sale. TV technicians from CBS were hauling thick, python-like cables out of their trucks, wheeling cameras onto the field, thirty of them in all. CBS had put thirty-two units of fifty-second commercial time on sale at $7,000 apiece last Tuesday, and all but four had been sold by Friday.

It was like an Ali–Frazier fight; it was like Carnaval. The game was scheduled to begin at 3:30 P.M., but so vast was Pelé's appeal that as early as 10:00 A.M. fans were lined up outside the ticket windows, and as late as 4:15 P.M. they were still trickling into the stadium. Meanwhile, throughout the entire first half, multilingual scalpers were asking—and getting—twenty dollars for a six-dollar ticket.

Pelé had traveled to the stadium two hours before kickoff, wearing a soft, red leather jacket over a white turtleneck jersey, flared brown slacks, and brown and white shoes. And sunglasses. And a smile.

He came in a Carey bus with his teammates, after consuming a pregame meal of steak, salad, fruit salad, and, of course, coffee.

"There were mashed potatoes, too," reported Pelé's faithful Boswell, Julio Mazzei, "but he didn't eat them."

Outside the stadium, several hundred fans, most of them South American, were queuing up, waiting for the ticket booths to open. None of them was aware that Pelé had arrived, because the bus had parked inside the wire fence at the open end of the old stadium. By the time they realized, Pelé was gone, walking through a long gray-and-white hallway, lighted by naked bulbs. But even those dismal surroundings couldn't cheapen the soft red leather jacket.

"He got that jacket in Istanbul a few weeks ago," said Mazzei. "It's sheepskin, very soft, like a glove. It cost him two hundred and ten dollars, in American money. He got three—one red, one white, one blue."

In the Cosmos' dressing room, as Pelé was putting on his green-and-white uniform, Mazzei said, "Since this is his first game, he feels that the American people

CHAPTER THREE

are looking to him to do something. It will be difficult because this is the first time he plays together with this team. But," Mazzei added forcefully, "he will try."

Outside, on the rim of the concrete horseshoe, American and Brazilian flags fluttered in the warm breeze. The crowd chanted Pelé's name as he stood at one end of a ramp beneath the stadium, not yet visible to them. Several dozen children, some with his picture or banners or balloons with his name, leaned far over the rail to see him.

Then, one by one the players ran out and were introduced, until finally it was Pelé's turn to take the field. The crowd rose as one, waving their Brazilian flags and screaming "Pelé, Pelé," as the dark figure with the number 10 on his back emerged, bursting up the ramp, his arms stretched over his head and the fingers of both hands forming "V"-for-victory signs. Confetti fell like snow, as Pelé turned slowly toward every section of the stadium, acknowledging the deafening cheers.

Then Pelé and Dallas's Kyle Rote, Jr. (son of the former New York Giants football star) exchanged Brazilian and United States flags. Two years before, Rote had catapulted to national prominence, winning both ABC-TV's Superstar competition, and the NASL's Rookie-of-the-Year award. Today, in the presence of Pelé, his fame was eclipsed.

But even while the fans cheered, experts were declaring their skepticism. "The average American sports fan might be disappointed because they'll expect Pelé to dribble the length of the field every time he touches the ball," warned Columbia University soccer coach John Rennie. "But they'll never see him do that. He's not a spectacular player with the ball," Rennie added. "You have to appreciate what he does *without* the ball —controlling and setting up the offense. He inspires other people to give up the ball, because they know he'll give it right back. Up to now, a lot of the Cosmos have been afraid to give the ball up, but there isn't a player alive who wouldn't give it to Pelé."

But up in the stands, neither Pelé's wife, Rosie, nor his brother Zoca seemed worried. "I'm so excited," said Zoca, once a player with Santos and now a lawyer. "I know my brother is happy he is here."

And then Pelé began the 1,254th match of his career, demonstrating from the outset some of the reasons for his exceptional popularity. (For three days during a war in Biafra, a special truce was declared to allow him to perform for both sides. A Nigerian army captain had escorted him halfway across the river separating warring tribes, turned him over to his Biafran counterpart, and saluted. No one could blame Pelé when the war resumed the day after he departed.) Today it took a full two minutes before Pelé touched the ball, but when he did, it was with the sinuous grace that had earned him his unparalleled reputation. Gently, he flicked the ball behind him to Alfredo Lamas, as the crowd roared. From then on, he passed with the accuracy of a preprogrammed computer. He controlled both the ball and the tempo of play. His

CHAPTER THREE

skills at dribbling the ball made the most fluid Dallas defenders look stiff, clumsy and awkward. Yet none of his maneuvers resulted in a goal. He was outwitting not only his opponents, but his teammates, too.

Then Dallas scored, on a breakaway by Alty McKenzie. Pelé told his teammates not to worry. As the Cosmos moved downfield again, Pelé barked instructions, using a system of hand signals to tell other Cosmos where to pass the ball, when to dribble, when one of the Dallas forwards was threatening to break loose. In the twenty-first minute, midfielder Johnny Kerr floated a ball across the Dallas goal mouth. Outleaping the taller Dallas defenders, Pelé headed the ball point-blank at the Tornado goal, but it bounced off one of the eight-foot-high white wooden goal posts. On two other occasions, Pelé laid the ball off expertly, once to Israeli Mordecai Shpiegler and once to Argentinian Julio Correa, but both shots were nullified by goalie Ken Cooper's acrobatic saves. As halftime approached, a long-time Pelé-watcher shook his head and said, "He can do nothing alone. He needs time. Two or three games."

Then, with six minutes left in the first half, Dallas scored again. At the end of forty-five minutes, a funereal hush had descended over the crowd.

"Even though we were down, 2–0, at the half, there was a feeling in the dressing room that we could still win," Cosmos coach Gordon Bradley recalled later. "Pelé kept telling us that we could come back. He was a big inspiration to us, and we came out charging in the second half."

With 12 minutes gone in that second half, using his right foot to dribble the ball as deftly as Nate Archibald ever dribbled with his right hand, Pelé suddenly stopped and lofted a soft pass right to the feet of Mordecai Shpiegler. Shpiegler shot and scored. Then, almost nineteen minutes later, Pelé soared high in front of the Dallas goal, seeming to hang momentarily in midair, and headed a high pass from Shpiegler into the far corner of the nets, tying the score at 2–2.

His fans gave him a rousing ovation. It was his first goal as a Cosmo; the 1,221st of his career. The game ended in that 2–2 tie, but that didn't matter. Pelé had thrilled a national TV audience and almost twenty-two thousand fans in Downing Stadium with flashes of genius.

Not that CBS's coverage of the match was an unqualified success. Entitled "The Return of Pelé," it was as frustrating as Pelé's performance was exciting. Wherever Pelé wandered, no matter who had the ball, the cameras focused on him and him alone. Even more frustrating than the camera's slavish addiction to the featured player were the inopportune commercials, which popped onto home screens with total disregard for the action down on the field. In sports like baseball and football, whose growth television had stimulated, commercials were squeezed into built-in lulls. But soccer is a continuous-action game. There are almost no time-outs, no substitutions. Play flows between the opposing goals, without the herky-jerky stop-and-go format that, as much as its mayhem, has made pro football the sport sponsors love best. So, while the Cosmos were scoring their first goal, set up by a pass from Pelé, CBS was selling its audience insurance. The instant replay that followed lacked, to put it mildly, a certain immediacy. Goals in soccer are scarce to begin with, and are usually preceded by a long build-up of tension. Missing that first goal left dyed-in-the-wool soccer fans as uptight as a teen-ager on a date with a nice girl who'll pet, but won't go "all the way."

Still, if CBS's coverage was something less than an artistic tour de force, it turned out to be a financial bonanza. For a one-shot, "The Return of Pelé" had scored big. The New York City ratings were 10.3 and 35 (in lay terms, that means 10.3 percent of all the sets in the area, whether turned on or off, and 35 percent of all those sets turned on). Most important, almost all the viewers who tuned in from the beginning stayed through to the end. "The Return of Pelé" had simply kayoed the offerings of New York's two other network channels, both of which had aired tennis matches.

"I'm not going to jump out of a window with joy," said CBS Sports Director Bob Wussler, "not on one show. But obviously it suggests to us a great deal of interest in The Man and his game."

Meanwhile, "The Man" was busy heaping praise on everyone. "I was pleased with the way they responded to my directions out there," Pelé said, in a noisy post-game press conference, held outside to accommodate the large contingent of American and foreign journalists. "In the games I saw them play before, they were outrunning the ball. This time the team played my type of game. They've started to let the ball run for them. And we'll be working on this even more in the next few practices."

For some of his more inexperienced teammates, Pelé spiced his praise with a pinch of caution. "They've got to learn to look for other players than me to pass to," he said. "I would like to see them dribble more themselves and if they have the shot, I want to see them take it. This takes time to develop," he added, "but I feel that we definitely have the talent on this team to be a good club."

The press conference ended with Pelé throwing his arms around Rosie and kissing her.

Later, as Dallas star Kyle Rote, Jr., left the stadium, he revealed what it felt like to play in Pelé's shadow. "There's nothing worse than standing up there while they're waiting for Pelé," he said. "To hear the fans yelling, 'Get outta here, ya bum, we want Pelé.'" Earlier, Rote had contrasted Pelé's multimillion dollar contract to the pittance paid almost every other player in the North American Soccer League. There existed, he claimed, a tacit agreement among franchise owners to limit total team salaries to $56,000. "That's about $3,000 per man," Rote told reporters. "I believe only two players on our team make more than $5,000 right now." Rote, only twenty-four years old, wanted to change all that, and more. "I want to see a brand new contract, a minimum salary, and three Americans in every starting lineup," said Kyle, who was the only American among the Tornado starting eleven.

"Now that we've gone from the era of the slaves to the era of the King," he added, "I don't want anyone to forget the slaves. They were the ones who built the pyramids for the king. I don't want anyone to forget all our free clinics and low salaries. Pelé's salary," he concluded, "is twice the sum of the combined salaries of everybody else in the league."

Then Kyle moved off toward the Dallas bus, elbowing his way through the crowd waiting outside the stadium for a glimpse of Pelé—a crowd larger than the total attendance for most NASL games.

4

The Greening of Pelé

THE SHORT, STOCKY BLACK MAN looked suspicious. He entered the airport in Salisbury, Rhodesia, carrying a suitcase, guarding it as if he were concealing something—maybe silverware he had stolen from a hotel.

"Open the case," ordered a customs official. The man clicked the catches, and the lid snapped up, and revealed $100,000 in ten neat piles.

After his arrest, the man explained that he was Pelé, the world's most famous, and richest, athlete. The money? Well, his soccer team, Santos of Brazil, was on an exhibition tour, and every time he played an exhibition game Pelé received $10,000 in cash.

CHAPTER FOUR

It was almost impossible to think of Pelé without thinking of money. If the astronomical sum he had received for signing with the Cosmos made other NASL players feel insignificant, it gave him instant glamour in the eyes of an audience who otherwise wouldn't have known a penalty kick from a throw-in.

But why, some people were wondering, would Warner Communications, Inc., a conglomerate that thrived on *The Exorcist* and The Rolling Stones, invest millions of dollars in what some would consider an over-the-hill thirty-four-year-old, and a team whose average attendance in 1974 was 4,700 a game, in a sport of unproven potential in the United States?

The answer was, Warner executives were confident they would have little difficulty recouping their investment, for the following reasons:

- If average attendance rose, as the Cosmos expected, from 5,000 to 20,000 for their forty home games over the next three years, the team's gate would increase by almost $3 million.
- Away from home, the Cosmos would get a percentage of any home-team ticket sales above and beyond the pre-Pelé average, which should enrich the Cosmos' coffers by another $750,000 over three years.
- With Pelé in their lineup, the Cosmos could gross $300,000 a year in international tours; without Pelé, the Cosmos probably wouldn't have any international tours.
- Besides playing for the Cosmos, according to his contract, Pelé would become a world-wide Warner

representative and work for the Warner-owned Licensing Corporation of America, which intended to garner as many Pelé endorsements as possible.

• If that long-awaited national TV contract for the North American Soccer League ever materialized, the Cosmos—because of Pelé—would be granted a much larger share of the TV income than any other team. Furthermore, Warner was making plans for Pelé to star in Warner-produced movies and television shows.

• Pelé could help soccer, and soccer could help Warner's cable TV division, which in 1974 grossed more than $30 million. "Three, four, five years down the road," a Warner executive explained, "soccer could be very important to us when pay cable comes into being on a wide scale."

Apart from any additional income Pelé generated, Warner would also benefit from depreciating the value of Pelé's contract, for tax purposes. "I don't think the Cosmos would have signed Pelé without the tax ramifications," said Bob Woolf, the attorney who represents many of America's most famous athletes. "It would have been too great a risk." Woolf estimated that if Pelé's contract were $4 million, Warner could write off $2 million in taxes, as long as it could prove to the Internal Revenue Service that it had lost money in other corporate divisions.

Finally, $4.5 million wasn't so extravagant a sum at all for a company that in 1974 alone earned $48.5 million on gross revenues of $720 million.

Nor was it, in fact, such a spectacular sum to Pelé

CHAPTER FOUR

himself. Until Pelé retired in 1974, Santos of Brazil was paying him an annual salary of $400,000, plus $10,000 for each of about forty exhibitions in which he appeared. On top of that, he received then—and was still receiving—another $200,000 a year from Pepsi-Cola, for which he devoted several months a year to staging clinics for youngsters and making personal appearances on Pepsi's behalf all over the world. Adding to that total the $200,000 a year Addidas sportswear paid him until 1974, plus other incidentals, his income on salary and endorsements alone approached the million-dollar mark. Nor did that figure include income from investments in the Amazon region of Brazil (yielding tax-free profits) or from fifty to seventy-five apartments in the Santos–São Paulo area, a company that sold his trademark, an import-export firm, $2 million worth of stock market shares, coastal real estate, a rubber factory, a travel agency, a clothing company, and a coffee company ("Cafe Pelé"), all of which brought him an estimated $1 million dollars more every year. At the time he retired, in fact, he was the largest individual taxpayer in Brazil, paying about $48,000 per month. He would meet twice a year with Brazil's tax minister to discuss what portion of his income was taxable.

But while everyone else chattered incessantly about Pelé's incredible wealth, the Brazilian himself was reluctant to talk about money, as if there was something undignified or vulgar about a king counting his gold coins in public. "I don't know how much I'm worth,"

THE GREENING OF PELÉ

he said. "My father told me that when you're working, don't stop to count your money."

Nor was his business manager, José Roberto Ribeiro Xisto, any more illuminating. Both Pelé and Ribeiro consistently dodged money specifics, pointing out that Pelé's promotional earnings were only estimates, anyway. Pelé did reveal that he would pay Brazilian income taxes. He also admitted, to no one's surprise, that he had already accumulated "enough money to live on" for life. But inevitably, he swung every financial discussion toward the various projects he intended to fund with his income from the Cosmos, including a cultural program for scholarships in soccer and other sports, in Brazil and in the United States, and the "Pelé Foundation," whose purpose would be to establish soccer schools in the United States. (In other words: tax shelters.)

Strangely enough, though, in Brazil, where resentment at Pelé's defection was still intense, part of the media were speculating that the only reason Pelé was playing in the United States was for the money—that he was in deep financial trouble. According to a leading columnist in the weekly magazine *Opinião*, for example, Pelé had been lured back into soccer by "nine million dollars . . . from the sky, for a man who literally is on the verge of bankruptcy." (The writer didn't enhance his credibility on this side of the equator by nearly doubling Pelé's actual payoff.)

In his daily column for the newspaper *O Globo*, Ibrahim Sued alleged that the revelations about Pelé's

CHAPTER FOUR

desperate financial plight came from a Brazilian banker. "Pelé lost plenty of capital on an unsuccessful business deal," Sued reported. "The Cosmos came at the right time."

Where there is smoke, says the old adage, there is usually fire; but this time, most observers agreed, what was drifting north from Brazil was probably just marsh gas. Pelé, when questioned, did admit to relatively minor losses in a rubber products investment, but scoffed at rumors he was in a serious financial bind. "I came out of retirement because I missed soccer and because I saw playing in the United States as the new challenge I needed," he insisted. "If I needed the money," he added, "why did I take so long to sign?"

The consensus among reporters was that a few Brazilians were turning a tiny truth into a big lie, out of the same resentment that led one newspaper to criticize Pelé for not appearing at a farewell game in Rio "for fear of being booed," and another newspaper to run a headline that exclaimed: "JUNE 9, BRAZIL'S FIRST DAY WITHOUT PELÉ."

On Wednesday, June 18, the Cosmos were scheduled to play the Toronto Metros-Croatia (the weird name was a compromise, embarrassing to a league anxious to escape its image of foreignness, between the NASL and the team's Croatian supporters). It would be Pelé's first league game, his official baptism as a member of the Cosmos—a club that was clutching

THE GREENING OF PELÉ

with raw fingers to third place in its division, a potpourri of mostly has-beens and never-weres, but with a few players of enormous potential. His job was to blend the sweet and the sour into a sauce he could stomach, a team he could play for with pride. Between the exhibition against Dallas and that league-opener against Toronto, Pelé turned part hypnotist, part conman, trying to convince his teammates that they *could*, that all they lacked was confidence, not skills. And, on the surface at least, he seemed to be gaining ground.

"Sunday was my birthday," said Tony Piciano, who was born in Argentina, and later played two years with Long Island University. "During the first ten minutes of our game against Dallas, I was overawed and nervous. But being on the same field with Pelé was the greatest birthday present I could have received. Pelé relaxed me. He told me to take it easy and play my game, and I'm really grateful to him, as are all the players."

"Pelé has certainly helped me, too," added goalie Sam Nusam, soft-spoken and catlike, a twenty-nine-year-old Bermudan who shared with Pelé a passion for fishing. Nusam had started out with Montreal four years ago, moved to Vancouver in 1974, then to the Cosmos the year after, replacing the NASL's bad-boy goalie, Shep Messing—a Harvard graduate whom the Cosmos shipped to Boston because he couldn't tailor his freaky ways and mod life-style to coach Gordon Bradley's conservative prescription for winning. "Pelé's not afraid to come back and help the defense

CHAPTER FOUR

clear the ball out of danger," Nusam explained. "And he gives me the confidence of knowing one mistake won't cost me the game anymore."

Later in the season, too many mistakes would cost Nusam his starting job, but right now he was ecstatic. Another convert to Pelé's positive thinking was Mordecai Shpiegler. Pelé, in the Cosmos' campaign for customers, was the charismatic candidate with broad national appeal. Shpiegler was the running mate who could wow them in the Bronx. The superstar of tiny Israel had joined the Cosmos only five games before, but had quickly turned into the team's most effective forward. A veteran of World Cup competition, once sought after by first-division English clubs, he was a true quality player, and Pelé took to him like Damon to Pythias, recognizing in him one of those unselfish players so necessary if the race of Pelés is to prosper.

Shpiegler was a player who firmly believed that to give was better than to receive, proof being the generous pass he had lofted on Sunday to set up Pelé's first goal as a Cosmo. Although the Brazilian and the Israeli couldn't communicate too well verbally, Shpiegler was giving his thanks in the one language every professional athlete understands. Earlier in that game, with a chance to score himself, Pelé had passed perfectly to Shpiegler, allowing the Israeli to score a goal, too.

"I'm very excited about playing with him," Shpiegler said before the Toronto game. "Now I know that when I make a cut, he's going to spot me and pass the ball to me. And I also know where he's heading, so I can pass the ball to him."

The understanding these two veterans had reached was clear: You scratch my back, I'll scratch yours—what coaches prefer to call "the team concept."

It was becoming obvious, too, that Pelé's success over the years was due as much to his personality as his performance: He had an uncanny knack for making supporting players feel *wanted*.

Mark Liveric was another case in point. Until Pelé, Liveric had led the Cosmos in goals, shots—and dates. He was the classic sports pretty-boy, a star as a teenager with Yugoslavia's National Junior Team—equivalent, say, to being an Olympic basketball star while still in high school. Liveric wore a shag haircut and the bottom button of his shirt open. At any Cosmos game, he could be seen counting curvaceous female bodies in the stands, as carefully as general manager Clive Toye counted the house for warm bodies. Liveric admitted he was slow adjusting to Pelé's style, but was determined to improve. "He's so good, you don't know where he's going with the ball and when he's going to pass it," he said. "But I'm beginning to understand how Pelé plays and also learning to know where the ball is going to go after he touches it."

What the Cosmos were learning, in fact, was that Pelé's qualities as a master tactician transcended even his uncanny skills at scoring. Cool, unruffled, even when being rushed, he had the ability to plot offensive strategies on the spur of the moment. At any in-

CHAPTER FOUR

stant, his intuitive radar told him the position of every other player on the field. Pelé's greatest talent wasn't scoring goals; it was turning eleven individuals into a team.

And every one of the Cosmos had his favorite memory of Pelé. For many, it was the 1958 World Cup competition, when fans throughout the world got their first glimpse not only of Pelé's awesome skills, but of his remarkable competitive drive. After sitting out the opening rounds with an injury, the seventeen-year-old Pelé came back in the quarterfinals to score the only goal in Brazil's victory over Wales. It is a goal soccer fans still talk about. His back toward the Welsh goal, Pelé, with his right foot, suddenly kicked the ball in a gentle arc back over his own ducking head. Then, as it bounced off a surprised Welshman (Pelé had developed a technique of banking shots off his opponents' bodies), he spun around and, with his left foot, sent the ball sizzling into the Welsh goal for the winning score—without the ball ever having touched the ground!

And then, in the semifinals, the seventeen-year-old was suddenly transformed into the man. France, the Brazilians' opponent, opened the match with a quick, stunning goal, one that put the favored Brazilians into shock. It was left to Pelé, the youngest of them all, to restore, if not his teammates' self-confidence, at least their pride. He gathered his team around him. He gave them a tough, yet inspirational, peptalk. Then

Pelé went scored three goals, single-handedly sending France to defeat.

In the finals, against Sweden, he was just as brilliant. Surrounded by opposing players and moving away from Sweden's goal, he let a pass bounce off his thigh, then, with a toe, hooked the ball over his head. While it was still in the air, he whirled to boot it past the astonished Swedish goalie, giving Brazil its first World Cup ever.

Even then, at seventeen, Pelé could dribble the ball through a crowd of players, easily sidestepping their futile tackles. The path of his passes was as perfect as any computer could program. His shots were so powerful, opposing goalies guarded their nets even when Pelé was sixty or seventy yards away, defending his own. He was accurate when he headed the ball, too, but—as his Cosmos teammates were now learning—his greatest asset lay within that head.

"A good player will be thinking maybe two moves ahead," says Gordon Bradley, who was promoted from head coach to vice-president after the season ended. "Pelé can think six or seven moves ahead."

On Wednesday, cynics who thought the Cosmos sellout for the Dallas exhibition was a fluke turned into instant optimists. The crowd filling Downing Stadium for Pelé's first league game, against Toronto, totaled 22,500—about 7,000 more than the Cosmos' management had anticipated, and a second straight full-house.

CHAPTER FOUR

While the fans chanted "Pelé, Pelé, Pelé," as fervently as a religious congregation invoking the name of their most powerful deity, Toronto coach Ivan Markovic—a Yugoslav who had stocked his roster with fellow countrymen—was briefing the press on his strategy for stopping Pelé. The briefing didn't take long, however. Markovic announced he had no special plans for containing Pelé at all.

"If we devote all our time to trying to stop him," Markovic reasoned, "then there's going to be other Cosmos wide open, and with Pelé's passes, he can really hurt you badly."

Meanwhile, in the Cosmos' dressing room, Pelé was telling a crowd of reporters, "I feel much better now that my first game with the Cosmos is under my belt. Tonight's game counts in the standings. It's for real, and I'm looking forward to the league competition.

"I think," he added, "that in the last two practices the team has slowed down its play, so now instead of running the ball, we're making the ball run for us."

It was the second time Pelé had used those exact same words. It wouldn't be the last. Ever since he had first donned a Cosmos uniform, Pelé had been trying to slow down the attack, to transform it into a semblance of the Brazilian model. The North American Soccer League tended to play English-style soccer, with long passes the length of the field, lots of physical contact, and every player a candidate for an Olympic marathon. It was a style that made more demands on a player's endurance and toughness than on his ball-handling skills. The Brazilian style, on the other hand, depended more on finesse—short pinpoint passes, ball control—on a slower tempo only expert ball-handlers could impose. The problem was that few of the Cosmos actually had the technique required to put Pelé's theories into practice. That Brazilian style was foreign to the rag-tag collection of NASL players—over-the-hill veterans from a dozen countries, promising youngsters from nations where proficiency in soccer was low (such as the United States), seasoned here and there with a handful of authentic world-class players, on vacation-with-pay from their first-division teams in England and Scotland and Italy and Argentina, and therefore not about to kill themselves trying.

As it turned out, though, to beat Toronto the Cosmos didn't need to be very proficient, anyway. Despite coach Markovic's mini-monologue about the dangers of concentrating too much on Pelé, his team did just that. "No matter what he said, I knew they were going to concentrate on me," said Pelé afterwards, "and before the game I told my teammates that they should look for the free man. I'm happy to say they did just that," he added, gloating over the Cosmos' 2–0 victory, "and we were able to control the pace of the game."

To illustrate just how closely he had been shadowed, he recalled a typical incident. "Once, when I was at midfield, they had two men on me, and I wasn't even in the actual play. So," he said, "I made a feint—and

49

CHAPTER FOUR

another Toronto player came over. Because of this, we had three men free near the penalty area."

In the Toronto dressing room, reporters had cornered Gene Strenicer, one of two defenders assigned to guard Pelé constantly. "The way he trapped the ball, and the way he was able to release the pass off to one of his teammates was something that you read about," marveled Strenicer. "But until you get the honor of playing against him, you can't believe the way he handles himself out there."

It was the honor of having Abdul-Jabbar block your shot ten times in a row, or Walt Frazier strip the ball from you every time you dribble downcourt; the "honor" a cornerback feels when Broadway Joe burns him for a touchdown pass, the honor a pitcher feels when he watches Hank Aaron blast his fastball out for a record-breaking 715th home run.

"I think he can do just about anything with the ball he wants to," Strenicer added. "He knows exactly where everyone on the field is at all times, and that doesn't include only his teammates. Once he saw that one of our defenders was going to intercept a pass near our goal, and he looked at this player's feet and headed to where the ball eventually was going. It's almost unbelievable, but I guess that's why they call him the best ever."

Pelé hadn't scored, missing, in fact, two close-up shots and a header in the first half. But he wasn't worried. "The ball here is softer and lighter than it is in Brazil," he said, "and if you hit it as hard as you do in Brazil, it's going to go off on an angle and take off over the bar. It will take some time, but I'll get my kicks adjusted to the ball."

What worried others, however, was whether his thirty-four-year-old body could still take the punishment meted out by NASL defenders. Some people think soccer is not a "contact sport." They change their minds when they see bodies flying like passengers in a car crash who neglected to fasten their safety-belts. "Throughout his career—eighteen years—he had very few injuries," said one observer close to the Cosmos. "And I can see an opposing coach here telling his team before a game: 'We're playing Pelé and he's here to help soccer, to help all of us, so let's play him honest, not dirty.' But what happens if Pelé makes fools of the other team in the first half? What happens in the second half?"

In the Toronto game, the referee had signaled four fouls committed against Pelé—two of them bone-jarring, body-block tackles. Still, Pelé said he didn't find the defensive coverage rough. "They were tough and that is just what I had expected them to be," he said. "After all, they were playing in a league game, and they wanted to win just as much as we did. But I don't think anyone really wants to go out there and hurt me."

Maybe not the players, but how about the fans? After the Cosmos' next game, against Boston, Pelé would change his mind.

5

A Rival—and a Riot

FOR ANYONE WHO DOUBTED that life is full of bittersweet ironies, in the contest between the New York Cosmos and the Boston Minutemen there was compelling evidence. At Boston University's 15,000-seat Nickerson Field, one of soccer's longest and most thrilling rivalries would be revived. For the first time in nine years, the two most renowned soccer players of the past decade would meet face-to-face.

Although Pelé reigned as King of Soccer for more than eighteen years, from time to time his rule was challenged. Sometimes the challenger was an older pro whose career overlapped Pelé's. Sometimes the contender was a younger pro whose career might out-

A RIVAL—AND A RIOT

last Pelé's. Of all the challengers, though, the one who came closest to toppling him was Eusebio, the "Black Panther," star of the Benfica team of Portugal. If Pelé was the king of world soccer from the 1960s onward, Eusebio was his crown prince.

Most of the reporters and fans who filed into the stadium that Friday evening were familiar with Eusebio's reputation, but not the uncanny symmetry between his life and Pelé's. While Pelé was a youngster kicking a sock stuffed with rags through the streets of tiny, poverty-stricken Três Corações, in Brazil, Eusebio—a year younger—was kicking a ball through the teeming, poverty-stricken alleys of Lourenço Marques, in Mozambique, East Africa. Pelé's father couldn't afford to buy him a ball. Eusebio had a ball, but no shoes. His family was so poor, he had to play soccer barefoot.

And then, one day when he was ten years old, he found in a garbage dump the most beautiful object he had ever seen. A soccer boot, worn and battered, but still intact. So he sat down in the hot Mozambique sun. He sat down beside a small mountain of decaying refuse, and laced on that precious boot. And even when he discovered it was impossibly tight, his joy didn't dwindle. From then on, the shoe and Eusebio were inseparable. Whenever his shooting foot swelled up from being bashed against a soccer ball, he would, proudly, put on that one shoe and loop the laces under his foot to hold it in place.

Pelé signed his first professional contract at the age

CHAPTER FIVE

of fifteen, in 1955. One year later, Eusebio, also fifteen, signed his first professional contract, with Sporting Club of Lourenço Marques. Pelé was given, as a bonus, a handful of coins. And Eusebio's bonus?

"I've read about some of the money that American athletes get," he told some journalists in 1975, when he was playing for the Boston Minutemen (on vacation-with-pay from Benfica). "But money didn't mean a thing to me at the time. I was just happy to get, as my bonus, my first pair of soccer boots."

Eusebio's performance on the soccer field for his East African club drew scouts from Benfica of Portugal, which purchased his contract. He became rated second only to Pelé, consistently among the top ten scorers in Europe, despite the fact that over the decade that followed he submitted his knees to surgery three times.

And it was in Pelé's absence, in the 1966 World Cup, that Eusebio offered the most potent challenge to Pelé's supremacy ever.

In their opening match against Bulgaria, Brazil won, 2–0. Both goals came from free kicks, one in the first half by Pelé, the other in the second half by his legendary teammate, Garrincha. Throughout, Pelé had been shadowed ruthlessly, and brutally battered, by a Bulgarian named Zhechev, with little protection from the English referee. Pelé still looked as resourceful as ever, but a French journalist, looking down from the press box, observed prophetically during that first

A RIVAL—AND A RIOT

match: "Pelé won't finish the World Cup. It's amazing he hasn't gone *mad*."

Pelé didn't go mad—and he didn't finish the World Cup, either. By the end of that opening match against Bulgaria, Pelé had suffered a knee injury that would sideline him during Brazil's second match, against Hungary. And with Pelé on the bench, the Brazilians were defeated—their first loss in World Cup competitions since 1954, B.P.—Before Pelé.

Meanwhile, with Pelé injured, Eusebio was putting on one of the greatest exhibitions ever witnessed in world-class soccer. He won the cash bonus of £1,000, as individual high-scorer, with nine goals in six games—four of them against the surprisingly strong North Koreans, who led the Portuguese national team, 3–0, until Eusebio, the Black Panther, started blasting away. Portugal won, 5–3, and four of those goals were scored by Eusebio.

After the World Cup tournament ended, with England the victor, fans who had watched the competition in person or on television, all over the world, began to call Eusebio the new King of Soccer. "I feel that calling me the new Pelé is very unfair, both for Pelé and for me," Eusebio protested. "To me, Pelé is the greatest player of all time. I only hope that one day I can be the second-best ever."

But few listened to his disclaimer. With Pelé once again healthy, a special international match was arranged between Pelé's Santos team and Eusebio's

CHAPTER FIVE

Benfica team. Ironically, that match—equivalent to the heavyweight championship of the soccer world—was held not in one of the great soccer capitals of Europe or South America, with their 100,000-plus stadiums, and their protective moats to keep rowdy fans from swarming onto the field and committing mayhem and murder. That long-awaited joust, pitting the King against the Pretender to his throne, was held in New York City, in Downing Stadium, where, almost a decade later, Pelé would wear the colors of the New York Cosmos.

The verdict after the match was nearly unanimous. Pelé had proved that at twenty-six he wasn't ready to relinquish his title. Pelé and his Santos team destroyed Eusebio and Benfica, 4–0, with Pelé contributing one goal and three assists. And as the lopsided contest neared its conclusion, he deftly robbed the ball off Eusebio's foot, saluted the Benfica star, and sped off the field.

"I told you not to discredit Pelé," Eusebio told the hundreds of reporters who gathered after the game. "He's still as great as ever, and he'll stay that way until he decides to retire."

Pelé had retired. And now Pelé had un-retired. A week ago, Eusebio had been signed, for $25,000, by the Boston Minutemen, for the remainder of the season.

Hubert Volsinger, coach of the Minutemen, was trying to resist the temptation that had seduced To-

A RIVAL—AND A RIOT

ronto. "It would be easy to stick two guys on Pelé and tell them to chase him all over the field," he was saying, moments before his team took the field. "But that's not what the people are coming here to see. We'll let Pelé express himself and take our chances."

In fact, though, it was "the people" who would express themselves, with a violence that echoed as far as Warner Communications' plush conference rooms. With 11 minutes left to play, the Cosmos were losing, 2–1. Then Pelé scored a goal, but the referee disallowed it because of a Cosmos' pushing foul.

Throughout the game, fans had been spilling out of the stands, crowding six-deep along the sidelines. The Minutemen had sold 23,000 tickets for a stadium with 15,000 seats. Worse, Boston had oversold the Cosmos on the extent of their security precautions, hiring only fourteen policemen and eight Boston University ushers to control the crowd. At halftime, with the field ringed by spectators, Warner vice-president Rafael de la Sierra had walked to the nearest police station to ask for extra protection. "I told the man in charge there were over twenty thousand people in the stadium," de la Sierra would say later, "and he said, 'But they usually play before three thousand. I'm sorry, but all my men are out doing other things.'"

The moment the referee disallowed Pelé's goal, those extra 8,000 fans charged out onto the field in protest. But when they got near enough to touch their hero, they couldn't resist trying for a memento. Knocking Pelé down, they ripped his shorts and his shirt, and pulled off his right shoe. They twisted his ankle and bruised his knee. Pelé was only saved from more serious injuries by his quick-thinking bodyguard, Pedro Garay, who reached Pelé only seconds after the mob. "When I reached him," Garay recalled, "they were trying to rip him apart, and he was going backwards. I said, 'Get down, it's Pedro,' and covered him with my body. When I had visited the stadium on Thursday," he added, "I suggested that we call the game off. But Cosmos officials felt that would be unfair to all the fans who had looked forward to this game for weeks and had bought tickets."

"We were very lucky," said a shaken Clive Toye. "When the crowd started mobbing Pelé, he kept his leg flexible. If he had kept it stiff, he probably would have broken a lot more than his leg."

"I was shaken up," Pelé said after the Cosmos had gotten him safely into their dressing room. "I was afraid I was going to die."

Eusebio was also taken out of the game, for his own protection, after that incident. "I thought they were going to kill Pelé. I feared for his life and for mine," he said.

According to Clive Toye, the Cosmos considered walking off the field and hopping the first plane back to New York. But after a long delay, the game began again, the Cosmos losing by a goal. "If we didn't return, we would have had a great risk of a full-scale riot," said Toye. "But one thing is for sure: We'll make sure the same thing doesn't happen elsewhere.

A RIVAL—AND A RIOT

Starting with our next game, against Rochester, we'll send the head of Warner security two days in advance, and if he's not satisfied, Pelé simply will not play." (A few days later, NASL commissioner Phil Woosnam ruled that the New York–Boston game should be replayed.)

The next day, Saturday, Pelé flew to Brazil, scheduled to return in time for the Cosmos' game in Rochester the following Friday. Pelé's reason for returning to Brazil that weekend was to escort his two young children to New York. But, once he was in Brazil, the subject of soccer in North America kept cropping up at every turn. With a characteristic blend of candidness and diplomacy, Pelé told interviewers for the newspaper O *Estado de São Paulo* that the Cosmos were still very weak, and that he might ask management to hire more Brazilian players. He added that he personally was very happy in New York, "because the officials of the Cosmos are keeping their word on every topic we discussed."

Asked whether he would rejoin the Brazilian national team for the World Cup competition of 1978 (World Cup tournaments are held every four years, with 134 nations competing), Pelé asked, naively: "Is it true that the sports confederation wants to call me? If it does call me, and I'm still in good form, it will be my pleasure to rejoin the selection. But we'd better wait and see," he added. "After all, we're still three years away."

When he wasn't being a diplomat, he was being a

recluse, escaping into his $600,000 mansion on a sidestreet in Santos—a house he cherishes so, he even designed the doorknobs. The mansion took three years to build, but was worth waiting for; within its walls, Pelé is able to simulate a normal, ordinary life. It contains a movie theater, with forty seats, for his wife, Rosie, who is considered an expert filmmaker and photographer. Adjacent to the theater is Rosie's professionally equipped darkroom. (There is, of course, nothing "ordinary" about having a movie theater in your house; but, like many other big celebrities, Pelé would never be able to do something so normal as take his wife and kids to the movies!)

While Rosie is splicing and editing, Pelé can usually be found behind the house on his own private soccer field, playing with his son and daughter, or with the entourage of well-wishers and intimate friends who have become his informal bodyguards. "He will stop and sign autographs almost any place," explains Clive Toye, "so his friends have to protect him."

Despite the opulent home and private soccer field, Pelé has always had a reputation for being tight with a cruzeiro. His four-car garage shelters one expensive automobile—a Mercedes—but Pelé prefers to drive one of two Volkswagens, or his Opel. (The Mercedes was a well-publicized gift from Germany that Pelé accepted only after extreme diplomatic pressure was applied—and with considerable embarrassment.)

He has the reputation for being frugal, but generous, too, especially toward his family, to whom he has always been loyal. During his years with Santos, for example, every day that he was at home he stopped in to say hello to his father, Dondhino, and his mother, Celeste. Annually he sent them a check for $2,000—a substantial amount in Brazil. The apartment house they lived in was a gift from Pelé, as was their car, and the car of Pelé's younger brother, Zoca, who, while playing for Santos, shared Pelé's house with him.

Nor was his generosity directed exclusively toward his family. He still allows poor families to live rent-free in several houses he owns in Três Corações, where he was born. Though throughout his career he has been known to drive a hard bargain for his services, in his last year with Santos, he wouldn't accept a cruzeiro. And his substantial earnings from exhibition matches ($10,000 cash per game) were all donated to charity.

"The secret of Pelé's success," says Julio Mazzei, "is that he is the same poor boy who came to play for Santos at sixteen. He has the gift of human dignity, of total dedication to his sport and to people around the world."

Many figures in the public eye flaunt a false humility. However, even the most skeptical Pelé-watchers have become convinced that Mazzei's praise has the ring of truth. And yet, this is the man who, for more than eighteen years, has been the world's most honored athlete, the model for most other men's dreams. Perhaps no man in modern history was ever con-

CHAPTER FIVE

fronted by so many temptations to arrogance. No man ever rejected them so completely.

In 1970, for example, when the Brazilian national team defeated Italy, 4–1, to win the World Cup in Mexico for an unprecedented third time, the nation erupted in what *Journal do Brasil* headlined as THE BIGGEST CARNAVAL IN HISTORY. Every street was clogged with processions of honking cars, samba bands and conga dancers, chanting, "Bra-*sil!* Bra-*sil!* Bra-*sil!*" In Rio, while air force jets swooped low over Copacabana Beach, fireworks flashed in the night sky like artillery shells. Brazilian doctors had publicly advised heart patients not to watch the game on television, but many did—and many died, from over-excitement. Some celebrators blew off their hands with firecrackers. Others were trampled to death in the streets.

During the celebration, in Brasilia, the capital, President Emilio Garrastazu Medici, a tough retired Army general, not famous for his sense of fun, actually walked out of his palace in shirtsleeves to join a crowd of young Brazilians who were dancing through the streets. Then he declared a two-day holiday, and invited Pelé and his teammates to share with him a victory lunch in his Palace of the Dawn.

As usual, of course, the center of attention everywhere was Pelé, who had scored one goal and set up two more in the victory over Italy. At twenty-nine, he had played on all three of Brazil's world championship teams, a feat that had turned him into a demigod in a land where "futebol" was a religion—for the masses of the people, a welcome escape from a dreary and impoverished existence. Brazil's dirt-poor black majority loved him as one of their own, one of the few who had ever succeeded in a nation ruled by a white minority. Victory had given them the opportunity to open their national safety valve—and to unleash "Carnaval." The flesh-and-blood personification of that spontaneous Carnaval spirit was Pelé.

It is this constant tension between being "The Man" whom millions adore, and "a man" who adores his privacy, that has forced Pelé to adopt his unique lifestyle. On the one hand, he has tried to remain accessible, to show the millions who need soccer to "escape" that he has not forgotten he was one of them. On the other, he has tried to preserve a small sanctuary of aloneness, for himself, his wife, and their two children. Without it, he could never enjoy the fruits of his own fabulous success.

"It has been proved medically that Pelé's peripheral vision is just way above an average man's," says Giora Breil, head of the Pepsi-Cola world-wide youth soccer program. "So even while Pelé is signing autographs, he is looking out of the sides of his eyes for a getaway route, in case the mob gets wild."

As that incident in Boston proved, for Pelé there is a thin line between being a man-of-the-people and a captive-of-the-people.

Pelé signs $4.7 million dollar contract with New York Cosmos to become the highest paid team athlete in the world. Wife Rosa looks on along with Clive Toye (center), Cosmos General Manager and Steven Ross (right), President of Warner Communications.

Making his first appearance in New York Cosmos uniform at Downing Stadium.

At Santos home, in trophy room.

A Brazilian postage stamp issued to commemorate Pelé's thousandth goal.

Pelé's portrait in the Black Hall of Fame.

The solid gold soccer ball presented to Pelé when he scored his thousandth goal.

Pelé and Rosa following their wedding, February 21, 1966.

With son Edson, daughter Kelly Christina and wife Rosa.

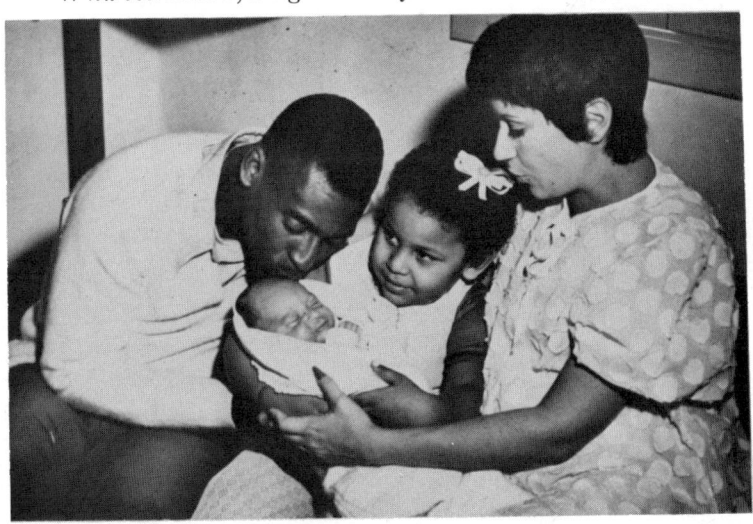

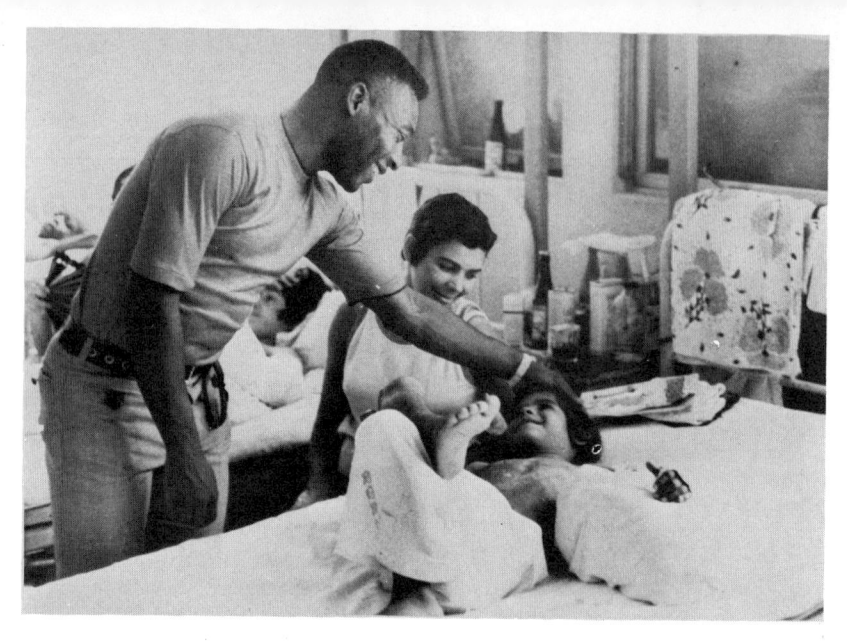

Visiting children's hospitals is a frequent occurrence in the life of Pelé.

With President Gerald Ford.

Pelé and Rosa receive a private audience with Pope Paul VI.

Pelé embraces Eusebio prior to game with the Boston Minutemen.

Celebrating World Cup triumph in 1970.

Pelé's famous "bicycle" kick.

IN ACTION

6

The King of England, the Queen of Hearts

IN ROCHESTER, on Friday, June 27, the Cosmos played the second of six straight road games—and five games in the next eleven days. The Cosmos' main concern was preventing a recurrence of the incident in Boston. "At first the Rochester people didn't understand our security requirements, but once we explained to them what happened in Boston, they agreed to comply fully with our demands," said Gordon Bradley. "I understand they've added security forces, so that there'll be more than eighty men on duty to handle the crowd. They've told us they expect a capacity crowd of twenty-two thousand and will stop ticket sales when that number of seats has been sold."

Pelé had flown into Rochester on Thursday, after leaving his daughter Kelly Cristina, aged nine, and his son, Edhino, four, with Rosie, in New York. Part of his early reluctance to come to the United States, once the Cosmos had made him an acceptable financial offer, was due to his fear that his children wouldn't be able to get adequate schooling in New York City. In their apartment-hunting, the Pelés' main concern had been to rent a place as near as possible to the one school that had impressed them—New York's prestigious, and private, United Nations School, renowned for its excellent academic program, and accustomed to dealing with the sons and daughters of diplomats and celebrities. Once Kelly and Edhino were enrolled, Pelé could feel secure. It wasn't easy to grow up like other kids when your father was one of the most famous men in the world.

The main defender of their privacy, of course, is Rosie herself. She has become adept at maneuvering herself and her children away from the spotlight that hounds her husband wherever he goes. Both she and Pelé are convinced that only if she can secure for the family a safe haven, away from the public's prying eyes, can they survive the enormous pressure of his fame. So jealous is Pelé of his private life, in fact, that before they were married in 1966, he and Rosie courted for six years in almost absolute secrecy. Both that courtship, and the wedding it led to, are classic examples of the Pelé style.

Pelé first met Rosemarie de Cholby when a contin-

CHAPTER SIX

gent of Santos players dropped in on a girls' basketball game one rainy afternoon. Rosie was a confirmed benchwarmer, and no matter how hard the laughing Santos players pleaded, her coach refused to put her in the game. Pelé really didn't mind at all; it gave him time to take a long, hard look at the girl he would eventually marry.

Rosie wasn't rich, but she wasn't desperately poor, either. Her father was employed by the harbor authority in Santos. She herself worked as a clerk in a record shop. Pelé—who plays the guitar, and composed two songs that became big hits in Brazil—suddenly decided that any record album sounded better when he bought it from Rosie. He began to stop by the store regularly. Soon they had fallen in love.

But during the six years that followed, Pelé never once took her out in public, and Rosie never once went to a stadium to watch him play soccer. According to Pelé, he was anxious to quarantine Rosie from the plague of female groupies that swarmed around him whenever he stepped out. According to some of Pelé's friends, the secrecy was necessary to Pelé for psychological reasons: He had to be sure that she wasn't a publicity hound like so many others, and the best way to make sure was to keep her away from his public. Few, however, are willing to suggest a third, and equally compelling, reason: Pelé is black and Rosie is white.

It wasn't until 1966 that Pelé and Rosie made their

first appearance together in public, and that was to announce that they intended to get married.

The furor this unexpected announcement caused was both energetic and predictable. From every newsstand, fan magazines blared exotic headlines about Pelé's love life, promising, as usual, a lot more than the stories inside delivered. Meanwhile, society columnists wasted reams of paper wondering what the guest-list for Pelé's wedding would look like, and where the great event could be held. One suggestion was that the ceremony take place in Santos' 35,000-seat stadium.

"If Pelé could have invited everybody he wanted to, the marriage would have been in a stadium a lot bigger," recalls Julio Mazzei. "He is an open-hearted man, you know. He would let everybody come. He would," adds Mazzei, "have been married with the ring in one hand and the pen in the other, signing autographs right through the ceremony."

But since Pelé couldn't invite everybody, he decided to invite almost nobody. He and Rosie were married in a simple ceremony in his parents' home. And only one team member, Pelé's best friend, Pepe, was invited to the intimate reception afterwards. Then he and Rosie left on a honeymoon tour of Europe, where friends in each country treated them like royalty, while keeping packs of reporters and fans at bay.

Now, years later, Rosie wears her dark hair cropped short, and prefers a conservative cut of clothing that permits her, in public, to blend softly into the background. "Rosie protects their private life like a guard dog," says Mazzei. "She is a very intelligent woman, with a good business sense, even though the final yes or no in everything belongs to Pelé."

Throughout Pelé's first season with the Cosmos, she politely refused to be interviewed by the press. And yet, wherever Pelé went, Rosie went, too—sitting, smiling, nervously puffing on a cigarette, waiting for the moment when Pelé would step out of the spotlight and they could start living again.

"I feel fit and am eager to see action," Pelé said before the game against Rochester. "Even though I didn't work out with the Cosmos this week, I did train with my old Santos club, and I feel sharp. I'm confident that we can avenge the 3–2 loss we had here against Rochester before I joined the club."

The Cosmos did avenge that defeat, winning 3–0. Pelé dribbled, he outleaped taller defenders. Playing slightly behind the forwards, and to the right side, Pelé sprayed the field with pinpoint passes. His ball traps, which he performed with his chest and his shins and any other part of his body he could get near the ball, even had some of the Lancers applauding. So it was only fitting that Pelé himself should score the first goal during this, the first game in which the Cosmos showed real cohesiveness since Pelé joined them. With thirty-one minutes gone in the first half, Julio Correa unleashed a low, hard shot that rebounded off the crossbar. Pelé, running up from twenty-five yards, headed the ball past the Rochester goalie, Perri, and into the nets.

"I still don't know where he came from," goalie Perri said after the game. "You can't take your eyes off him for a second. I've played against top forwards in my life," he added, "but believe me, there is only one Pelé."

When he said, "there is only one Pelé," Perri meant that it was not simply Pelé's ability to score goals and orchestrate attacking patterns that convinced critics he was the best ever. Perri was talking about the *art* with which Pelé executes those goals and tactics. For example, in a one-sided match between Santos and the Juventus team, in 1959, two members of Santos passed the ball forward along the sideline, then shot it toward Pelé, who was waiting in front of the goal. He lifted his right leg in a short, quick motion. He looped the ball over one defender's head. He ducked past that defender and lifted the ball again, as two more defenders approached. The ball seemed to pause in midflight, as Pelé feinted to his left; then he lowered his shoulders and dove between his opponents. Before the startled Juventus goalkeeper could react, Pelé had snapped the ball into the nets with his head. It was, historians of soccer insist, very close to that elusive "perfect goal."

Another example occurred in October 1962, when Santos played Benfica for the Intercontinental Cup—the world championship of professional clubs. On one play, Pelé took a pass from a teammate near the enemy

CHAPTER SIX

goal and booted it with a foot-first lunge that propelled him into the nets with the ball. Another time, he dribbled quickly downfield, but far to the right of the goal. Then, seemingly trapped in an impossible spot on the goal line, he got off a kick to the left while on the dead run. The ball flew straight to the foot of an advancing teammate, who tipped it in for a goal. All told, Pelé scored three goals that day, and passed for two others, giving Santos a 5–2 victory.

Or, also in 1962, when the Brazilian national team won the World Cup, under the leadership of Pelé. Pelé broke away, sprinted almost the length of the field, reversed his direction like a wide-receiver in football running an end-around, then slipped past two defenders and gently nudged the ball into the upper righthand corner of the nets.

Or, in Brazil's first match of the 1966 World Cup competition in England, when Pelé was awarded a penalty shot against Bulgaria. Four stocky Bulgarians stood shoulder-to-shoulder, their arms locked, in front of the goal, forming a seemingly impregnable wall. Pelé merely curved the ball around them and into the nets.

After beating Rochester, the Cosmos were jubilant. When Pelé arrived, they were in third place in their division. Now, with their win over the Lancers, they had edged into first place. Not only had Pelé proved that he was still capable of playing better than anyone else in the world, he had proved his special magic was contagious.

The next morning, the Cosmos flew to Washington by commercial jet, all except Pelé, who traveled in a private jet owned by Warner Communications. Then, while his teammates were lolling around the lobby of some nondescript hotel, Pelé was quickly shuttled to One Pennsylvania Avenue, to meet with President Gerald Ford. This was, in fact, Pelé's second visit with an American President, the first having been with Ford's predecessor, Richard Nixon. Pelé was grateful that American Presidents neither inherited their positions nor ruled by "divine right." The last time he had tangled with royalty, it had taken a corps of diplomats to sort out the proper protocols. It was in Brazil. And in Brazil, of course, Pelé is a King.

In 1962, Britain's Duke of Edinburgh paid an official visit to Brazil, and asked to see Pelé play so that he could compliment him personally, either before or after the game. For days the Brazilian foreign office grappled with a dilemma: Should the prince step down to the field to greet Pelé, or should Pelé step up to the tribune of honor to be praised by the prince?

To the relief of diplomats on all sides, the problem was resolved by Philip himself. Before the game, he went down to the field in São Paulo's Pacaembu Stadium to shake hands with Pelé. And afterwards a Brazilian journalist wrote: "In the Kingdom of Soccer, to whose territory all of the states of the world belong, the only King is Pelé. Above his majesty only the spiritual power of Heaven can rule."

The rhetoric may have been a bit overblown, but

CHAPTER SIX

Brazilians everywhere shared the basic sentiment: To hell with royalty; long live Pelé!

When Prince Philip had asked to meet Pelé, it was the equivalent of a foreign dignitary in the United States asking to be shown the Lincoln Memorial. After all, in Brazil Pelé had been accorded the status of a "national treasure." When Gerald Ford asked to see Pelé, it was with a blunter, more practical purpose. He was trying to boost the popularity of soccer in America. Undoubtedly Ford, a former college athlete himself, was aware of Pelé's fame and prestige. If he wasn't, Henry Kissinger probably briefed him. While the Cosmos were trying to get Pelé's signature on a contract, Kissinger had sent a telegram to Pelé, asking him to accept the Cosmos offer in the interest of bettering relations between Brazil and the United States.

When they met, Ford told Pelé: "I'm sure your presence will increase American interest in soccer. We have a lot of young people who are now learning to play. Eventually," he added, "we may be able to compete in world championships." (In fact, the United States had been competing in the world championship of professional soccer—the World Cup—since its inception, in 1930.)

Then Ford, dressed in a gray business suit, and Pelé, wearing a blue-and-red striped white suit, with flared trousers and gleaming white patent-leather shoes, took a ball presented by the Washington Diplomats of the NASL, and went outside to kick it around. Pelé tossed the ball into the air. He showed the President how to keep it alive simply by batting it from his head to his foot, from his foot to his head. Then Ford, star center of the University of Michigan Rose Bowl football team some forty years ago, and perhaps the most athletic President ever, took the ball out of Pelé's hands and tried to imitate him.

"Clumsy, clumsy!" the President chided himself playfully, as the glistening white ball glanced off his polished black shoes and bounded crazily away. "Maybe I could hit it better with my head than with my foot." Then the President added in a very loud whisper: "I'd center one for you, American style, but not with all these people looking."

It was a staged event—what the cultural historians like to call a "pseudo-event." If the Washington *Post* had been a company that delivered packages, instead of packaging the news, it never would have occurred. Still, it did show the Charlie Finleys, and the Jack Kent Cookes, and the Wellington Maras—fat-cat owners of franchises in American pro sports—that Pelé, and thus soccer, was an upstart to be reckoned with.

And that visit also showed how deeply Pelé was committed to promoting the growth of soccer in the United States, for there are no two things Pelé distrusts more than politics and religion (even though he is a devout Catholic). Given his choice, he would rather not meet in public with presidents and prime ministers and princes. He fears them for the same reason some suggest he feared making his courtship with Rosie public. He is afraid that people with power will try to use him for their own ends.

"If a prime minister or a king wishes to meet me," he says, "I gladly go to the palace for lunch or some talk. But I do not mix with politics or religion.

"I am Brazilian, but I feel everywhere at home," he adds, explaining, without personalizing, why he has turned down telephone calls from both Eldridge Cleaver and Muhammad Ali.

Mazzei sums up Pelé's understanding of his role a different way. "When Pelé is in Spain," says Mazzei, "the people there believe he is Spanish. When he is in England, they feel he is English. Russia, Yugoslavia, Turkey, France—it's all the same. Pelé is not an athlete, he is an international phenomenon."

In Hong Kong, for example, Pelé and some friends went to the edge of the city, where the British crown colony borders on Red China. Two Red Chinese border guards put down their submachine guns and crossed a no-man's-land of buffer zone to shake his hand.

They could have been shot.

7

What Makes Pelé Pelé?

THE LARGEST CROWD in the history of the North American Soccer League—35,620—packed RFK Stadium to see Pelé, including several hundred Brazilians, who waved their national flags and Santos banners, and never stopped shouting, "Pe-*lay!* Pe-*lay!*" Pelé didn't disappoint them. Sometimes he was the virtuoso—outrunning, outdribbling, outwitting and outshooting every other player on the field. His first (and the Cosmos' fourth) goal came on a shot from twenty-five yards out. Winger Jorge Siega passed the ball to Pelé near midfield. Pelé began leisurely dribbling forward, when he noticed that the Diplomats' goalie, George Taratsides, was fractionally out of position,

CHAPTER SEVEN

a little too far to the left side of his goal. Without altering that leisurely pace, Pelé suddenly cocked his foot and kicked, sending the ball curling into the upper righthand corner of the nets.

Pelé's second goal came off a rebound from a shot by twenty-six-year-old Manoel Maria, who had played sporadically with Pelé at Santos, and whom the Cosmos had just signed on Pelé's recommendation. With the Cosmos leading by the incredible score of 8–2 (like a 20–5 baseball game), Maria, a winger, moved the ball to one sideline, and with no angle whatsoever, simply blasted the ball at the Diplomat goalie's chest. The implication was clear—Maria was telling Taratsides he didn't *need* any angle to score off a goalie whose skills were so meager. He had reason to be arrogant, of course. About ten minutes before, he had tried the same tactic and had scored.

This time Taratsides managed to get his hands on the ball, but couldn't hold it. The rebound went to Pelé, in front of the goal. As he had with Cosmos goalie Sam Nusam, that first day of practice, Pelé passed up the chance to blast Taratsides's head into the goal along with the ball. He merely flicked the ball into the nets, out of the goalie's reach.

When Pelé wasn't being the virtuoso, he was being the choreographer, moving his players around the field with hand signals, creating attack patterns at midfield, and opportunities around the goal for Mordecai Shpiegler, Julio Correa, and Joey Fink—the young and talented homebred striker whom Pelé had replaced in the Cosmos' lineup at the beginning of the season.

Overall, Pelé scored two goals and assisted in two others. Everyone agreed that it was the best game the Cosmos had ever played in the history of the franchise.

In the visitors' locker room afterwards, Pelé sat on a stool, signing autographs for the group of kids crowding around him. Suddenly Pelé looked up and was surprised to see one fan who towered over all the rest. Pelé motioned for him to come forward. He signed not one, but three autographs for him, and then hugged him.

"I've never asked an athlete for his autograph before in my life," said Roy Wilner, the Diplomat defender who had spent a frustrating afternoon attempting to guard Pelé. "But after what he put me through, I just had to get his name on the game program. He's not only the greatest soccer player in the world," Wilner added, "he's one of the finest men I've ever met."

Wilner then explained to reporters why his afternoon had been so frustrating. "Since our coach told me last week that he was putting me on Pelé, I've had a lot of suggestions on how to stop him," Wilner said. "I got hold of some game films and studied his moves, trying to spot a weakness. Believe me, it's useless. There's no way to stop the guy without knocking him out, and I'm not that type of player.

"Twice I thought I had him stopped before he was able to start downfield," the twenty-five-year-old former Junior College All-American recalled, "and both times he made me look like a fool. Once he went right around me, and the other time he feinted in one direction, went the other way, and I found myself bumping into one of my own teammates.

"I've never seen a guy jump so high without running," Wilner added. "I'm five-foot-seven, which is one inch shorter than him, and I've been proud of the way I handle guys around my size. But he's got the best spring in his legs I've ever seen."

As Pelé left the stadium, several hundred kids were clinging to the fence outside, chanting his name. "That," said Pelé, "is the future of soccer in this country, not us."

"The children," said Julio Mazzei, as he watched Pelé walk toward the fence to sign even more autographs, "the little ones who have never seen him play, are drawn to him. They come calling Pe-*lay*, Pe-*lay*, to touch him, to be near him. They have no fear of him. A long time ago," he added, "I realized that it will never be possible to say what makes Pelé Pelé."

What does make Pelé Pelé? It was a question reporters were asking more and more, as it became clear that, even at thirty-four, the Brazilian could still make the incredible seem easy. Undoubtedly, in part the answer lay in Pelé's physical attributes. Medical tests have revealed, for example, that, when he is training, Pelé's heart beats fifty-six to fifty-eight times a minute. The heart of an average athlete beats ninety to ninety-five times a minute. Pelé can recover from an exhausting run within forty-five to sixty seconds; it takes other athletes much longer. His peripheral vision is 30 percent better than most other athletes'.

But other differences between Pelé and his competitors aren't so well hidden. Leonardo da Vinci once drew a man with his arms and legs outstretched, touching the inner perimeter of a circle, to show how perfect a man's proportions could be. Had Pelé been his contemporary, da Vinci probably could have used him as a model. Pelé's feet are absolutely parallel. The bone in his heel is so big and strong, it forces him to lean forward as he runs, and acts like a shock-absorber when he lands hard, after executing a high kick, or jumping to head or trap the ball.

Not only can Pelé run faster than most soccer players—100 meters in eleven seconds—he can jump higher, too. He can jump higher, and hover longer in the air, an attribute that allows him to jump *earlier* than most defenders, giving him a vital split-second advantage.

While the Brazilian national team was preparing for the 1966 World Cup, Pelé was miles away, in a university laboratory. His legs, arms and head were wrapped in wires, in a series of tests that were repeated off and on for three weeks. The results never varied. "They showed," said Dr. Hilton Gosling, an eminent Brazilian psychologist, "that whatever field of endeavor this man entered—physical or mental—he would be a genius."

"If properly trained," says Julio Mazzei, "Pelé could

still be one of the world's ten best in the decathlon. He can, for instance, play volleyball and basketball magnificently."

But other athletes could run as fast, jump as high, their bodies near-perfect, their internal organs incredibly efficient. Still, there was only one Pelé.

"The great, great star, the genius—whether he is a sportsman, a scientist, or a poet—is at bottom a simple man," says Mazzei. "Greatness is in simplicity, not complication." Mazzei sees an athlete as a triangle. The top third is the area of "specialty," a man's mastery of his craft. The middle third consists of his talent, plus his willingness to work hard in training, to keep his body in condition. The bottom third, the wide base of the triangle, consists of "human" qualities—integrity, personality, humility, ethics.

"There are those who have two or three great seasons, then they disappear," says Mazzei. "What happens? They are deficient in some area of the triangle. Often," he adds, "it is in the base. They do not possess depth of character to take their gifts higher and higher, so their gifts erode."

For almost nineteen years, Mazzei points out, Pelé has been the indisputable king of soccer. Throughout those years, his "human" qualities have remained intact. At the peak of Pelé's fame, Carlos Alberto, the captain of Santos, probably summed up why Pelé is Pelé better than anyone else, when he said, "If I need a soda, Pelé gets it for me."

WHAT MAKES PELÉ PELÉ?

"I believe that you can communicate not only with words," Pelé himself says, "but with actions, too. The way you behave is communication. I have always believed that, and tried to live by it. I have always believed that no matter how much fame a man has, he should live a simple life."

But he refuses to confuse "simplicity" with false modesty. "People say I have a little bit of everything," he says, when asked to explain why Pelé is Pelé. "But it is a little difficult to explain, the same way it is difficult to describe what Chopin had . . . what made Chopin what he was . . . what makes anybody? That is what made me."

When pressed to be more explicit, he adds, "My talent is a gift of God—I am only what He made me."

He is a devout Catholic. It is his religious belief that permits him to be humble, and, at the same time, accept his own genius. He is convinced that his talent is "the gift of God, and the willingness to be a perfectionist."

"I feel the divine gift to make something out of nothing," Pelé says. "You need balance, and speed of mind, and strength. But there is something else that God has given me. It's an extra instinct for the game. Sometimes I can take the ball and no one can foresee any danger. And then, two or three seconds later, there is a goal. This doesn't make me proud, it makes me humble, because it is a talent that God gave me."

Pelé believes that God gave him his talents; but,

CHAPTER SEVEN

more important, that God also gave him the perseverance to work at perfecting those talents. "To perfect his soccer," says Giora Breil, head of the Pepsi worldwide youth program, "Pelé took geometry lessons and learned how to play chess." The kid who couldn't finish grammar school knew he had to educate his mind as well as his feet.

And because he believes his talent is a gift from God, he has been careful not to misuse the power it has brought him. He has had to keep in mind that although his talents may, in comparison with other men's, seem godlike, he himself is mortal—destined, like the rest of us, to die and eventually be forgotten. "I cannot afford to err," he says, "because many people use me for an example. But I am human, and I am obviously capable of error. The biggest fear that I have is to be something that is beyond my capacity."

To counteract the world's tendency to deify him, Pelé has been careful to keep his perspective, aware that he is not only a man, but a *black* man. About ten years ago, at night, before a road game, the Santos team rented five taxicabs to take them to a motel, where they were to gather before traveling. Four taxicabs arrived. The one that was supposed to chauffeur Pelé and two teammates didn't.

Hours later, Pelé and his two teammates arrived in a private car. The cab had broken down, Pelé explained. "Well, why didn't you just stop the first car that came along?" Mazzei remembers asking him.

Pelé paused before he answered. Then he said, "Professor, can you imagine three black boys hitching at night? Do you think somebody would stop?"

When the cab broke down, Pelé and his teammates had approached every car that stopped for a traffic light nearby. It was hours before one man finally agreed to give them a ride.

"I can't understand it," Mazzei told him. "No one in all of Brazil would turn down Pelé."

Pelé looked at him, smiled slightly, then turned away.

It was then Mazzei realized: He hadn't told anyone his name.

8

Clive Toye's 75,000-Mile Odyssey: The Signing of Pelé

LOS ANGELES. Smog city, sprawl city. The American Dream was born here, swaddled in strips of glossy celluloid. Home of Clark Gable and Betty Grable, Gloria Swanson, and a million early swan songs from pretty young things lured in off the prairies by glittering marquee lights. The stepping-stone for a lucky few, a dead end for multitudes more. In this city where dreams may be either realized or brutalized, but are always merchandized, a cold breath blew down from the hills and touched the New York Cosmos. In tiny El Camino Junior College Stadium, before a capacity crowd of 12,176, the Los Angeles Aztecs defeated the Cosmos, 5–1. It was the first defeat for the New York team since Pelé had arrived, five games before.

Pelé missed five chances to score—the first in the fortieth minute. The closest he came was in the closing minutes of the second half, when one of his acrobatic scissors-kicks went wide by inches.

But the Cosmos didn't lose because Pelé was inaccurate in close. They lost because Pelé and the other attackers didn't get in close often enough. For the first time that season, the Cosmos' defense, regarded till then as the best in the league, collapsed completely. Pelé spent most of the game around his own goal, trying to help defenders blunt the Aztecs' relentless attack.

"Our defense made a lot of foolish mistakes against the Aztecs," said coach Gordon Bradley, the slim, thin-faced Englishman who had coached the club from its beginnings, and who, up to this year, had sometimes played as a defenseman. "They were coming up too far on attack and then having trouble getting back in time to stop the breakaway style of Los Angeles. If they were able to come back in time, they were out of gas, and weren't able to properly challenge the opposing forwards.

"The way we played was very disappointing," he added. "It seems that everything we were able to build up since Pelé joined us went down the drain in one game, but I really believe it's only a temporary setback. The boys realize the importance of our next game—a televised game, against Seattle. I've talked to

CHAPTER EIGHT

the defense and made it clear to them what I expect them to do, because Seattle can kill you with the same type of breakaway plays that Los Angeles used against us."

The next day, the Cosmos traveled to Seattle, to face the Sounders and their second nationwide TV audience.

When, on June 15, Pelé had made his debut on TV, commercial interruptions had prevented viewers from seeing the build-up toward one goal and most of the action leading up to another. "This time," announced NASL commissioner Phil Woosnam, "there will be thirty-second time-outs on goal kick situations to permit commercials. It usually takes fifteen to twenty-five seconds for a ball to be retrieved and placed into play on a goal kick," he explained. "Stopping the clock on those goal kicks for commercial use would provide the least interference with play. This is only an experiment," he added, "and we'll have to see how it works out."

Coach Gordon Bradley had his own problems—and not just finding a finger thick enough to plug up the Cosmos' suddenly porous defense. He was in danger of getting a cauliflower-ear, not from being cuffed, but from being conned. Ever since Pelé had joined the team, Bradley had spent hour after hour with a telephone receiver clamped to his ear, listening to foreign players who wanted a piece of that sugar-coated American soccer pie. "Before we got Pelé," he said, "we would get a few calls from foreign players a week.

THE SIGNING OF PELÉ

Now it seems that everyone who feels he has the ability to play for us is getting in touch with me.

"One day last week," he continued, "I got a call from Mexico, from a player who claims he's in the first division. I knew the call was costing him a lot of money, so I tried to keep the conversation short. But he started reading me off his credentials—and I think we talked for about twenty-five minutes.

"I went back to my desk, and within the next hour I got calls from players in Brazil, Portugal, and Argentina. I would say," he concluded, "that since Pelé joined us a couple of weeks ago, we've gotten over one hundred calls from overseas. We've gotten calls from Nigeria, Russia, Syria, Italy, Afghanistan, West Africa, Trinidad, the Virgin Islands, Honduras, Yugoslavia, Ghana, and even one from Hong Kong."

But foreign veterans weren't the only ones harassing Bradley. Young American amateurs were, too. "Back home, we've had to put a fence around the field," he said, "and we're always chasing the non-team-members off the field—some of whom get there long before we do. Then we'll notice that while we're doing our warm-up exercises on the field, they'll be doing the same drills outside of the fence. When we start running around the outer fringes of the field, they run their laps along with us."

Besides attracting old and new players, Pelé was attracting old and new money to the league. For example, Pelé's debut against Dallas so impressed a group of wealthy Mexicans, they immediately initiated nego-

CHAPTER EIGHT

tiations with the NASL to buy an expansion franchise in Houston. In 1971, Warner Communications had purchased their franchise for $25,000. New owners would have to hand over $500,000. And according to the NASL, they should consider that fat sum a bargain.

"Everyone is trying to get in on the action before the price skyrockets," one NASL official alleged. "The next time we expand, a franchise will cost a million." Next year, the NASL was planning to add four new franchises, expanding its total to twenty-four. By 1980, the league expected to have thirty franchises. The reason the league was inching forward from stagnancy to success in a single season, of course, was Pelé. But someone else deserved at least a moderate share of the credit. After all, right now Pelé would probably still be sitting in Brazil, counting coffee-nuts and profits, except for the Cosmos' general manager, Clive Toye. In luring Pelé to the United States, when hundreds of the most famous soccer teams in the world had tried to get his signature on a contract and had failed, Clive Toye had pulled off perhaps the greatest coup in the history of professional sports. So it didn't surprise anyone to learn of rumors printed in the Italian press that two of the teams that had tried to sign Pelé, Inter-Milan and Milan, were now trying to sign Clive Toye as their general manager.

"I know nothing about it," Toye said. "Someone sent me a telex about it, but I think it went to the wrong place. It just couldn't be me they're after."

THE SIGNING OF PELÉ

Clive Toye is an expatriate Englishman, with the face of a cherub and the conversational gift of a talk show host. An ex-sportswriter for the London *Daily Express*, his colleagues on Fleet Street reacted strongly when he announced he was emigrating.

"They thought I was bloody mad," Toye says. "They thought I was stark, raving, bloody mad, they really did. Y'know, here I was, chief soccer writer with thirty years of safe, solid employment ahead of me, plus all those trips abroad with the English team —and I'm telling them I'm going to *America*, for chrissake! To promote *soccer*, for chrissake!"

Toye started in the United States as the general manager of the old Baltimore Bays, moved to the NASL as its director of administration, then took over the Cosmos in 1971 when the team was organized. In those, the New York Cosmos' dog days, the only full-time professionals were washed-up "mercenaries of soccer" (Clive Toye's phrase), imported to stub their much-traveled toes against America's massive indifference. The squad worked out twice a week, and played its home games on Saturdays and Sundays. In their first year in the league, the Cosmos played in Yankee Stadium. The few fans who paid to see them were hypercritical first- and second-generation Germans and Italians, whose primary allegiance lay with local ethnic semipro teams.

"We could have put 40,000 people in Yankee Stadium anytime," Toye says. "All we had to do was schedule, say, a team from Italy, like Lazio. The only

CHAPTER EIGHT

problem was, we'd have 40,000 people cheering 'Lazio! Lazio!' "

After that first season, the Cosmos dribbled out to Hofstra University (which they still sometimes use for midweek practices), whose grotesquely bowed Astroturf also supported the New York Jets football team, in preseason training. But Hofstra, with its 13,600 capacity, in no way resembled a major-league facility.

Still, even more than a decent stadium, until the team moved to Randall's Island this year, they needed cash customers. At Hofstra, tickets sold for six dollars, four dollars and two dollars. The Cosmos had to average 7,500 paid-attendance to break even, but attendance at home games never climbed much above 5,000.

"We'll do anything we can to get a person inside a soccer stadium for the first time," Toye said at the time. "If we can get just enough people to take one look, then some of them will come again. They'll bring a friend because they enjoyed it. The snowball starts rolling."

As bait to entice local fans, the Cosmos dished up a promotional stew salted with give-aways and group rates. One Sunday against Atlanta, for example, 2,000 kids were handed free soccer balls. The Cosmos dealt T-shirts with the Cosmos decal to Junior and Sis, bumper stickers to Dad, and pennants to Mom. Against Finn Harp of the Irish Republic, in 1973, anyone who dressed up as a boy scout could talk his way into the stadium for fifty cents. A match against Montreal was billed as "Burger King Night with the Cosmos": Buy at any Burger King franchise and collect a discount ticket-voucher. At a game against St. Louis, every patron got a free record album.

But still fans resisted, by the thousands, the temptation to watch second-rate performers play the world's number-one sport.

One of the few converts Clive Toye did make, however, later proved instrumental in Toye's effort to latch onto something even blasé Americans might find irresistible—the legend named Pelé. In 1966, Toye, still a sportswriter for the *Daily Express,* wrote an article on the burgeoning soccer movement in America. Phil Woosnam read that article, was intrigued by it, and asked Toye for advice on how he could participate. Two years later, when the North American Professional Soccer League collapsed, and the survivors formed the NASL, they chose Phil Woosnam as their first commissioner, a position he still holds.

Woosnam was born forty-two years ago, in the mountainous farm country of Caersws, Wales. As a youngster, he was a standout soccer player, but he gave up the game because it interfered with his studies. He went on to university, eventually obtaining a graduate degree in physics. Then he taught for a few years and spent two more in the Royal Artillery.

Then he did what few players had ever done before him. At the age of twenty-four, he started playing soccer again—and in a few short months had reached the top rank of British football, playing midfield for West Ham United, then Aston Villa—both in En-

CHAPTER EIGHT

gland's vaunted First Division. When his career in British soccer ended, his career in American soccer began.

"The period of 1969 to 1973 was purely one of survival," says Woosnam of his first years as commissioner of the NASL. "We were trying to blend all of the forces to make soccer a success. It was a question of staying power. No one gave us a chance in 1969. But it wasn't all over as long as we had Lamar Hunt and Bob Hermann aboard."

Hunt is the Texas oil millionaire who broke the back of the NFL establishment in 1959 by starting his own football league, the AFL. Hermann is a St. Louis entrepreneur who has the Busch beer money behind him. They were the original owners of Dallas and St. Louis, now the only charter members left in the league. Hunt, who also owns the Kansas City Chiefs football team, in particular has given the NASL an aura of respectability it could not have obtained otherwise. Investors feel that if Lamar believes in it, it must be okay.

Like Hunt's AFL, which managed to survive its first year mainly on the strength of a TV contract, the NASL had television in the early days, and while it was a commercial bomb, Woosnam insists that the exposure generated new interest among kids across the country, especially in the suburbs of some of the larger cities. But to stir that vague interest into a mania, the NASL needed something more. The NASL needed Pelé.

THE SIGNING OF PELÉ

Sometime in the spring of 1975, Clive Toye was sitting in his room at the G.B. Motor Inn, not far from the Brussels airport in Belgium. He looked up, through the open door, and into the room across the hall from him. A chambermaid was carefully arranging a bouquet of roses.

"Who are they for?" Toye called out.

"For the King," the chambermaid replied.

"The king?" Toye asked, wondering what Belgium's King Baudouin might be doing at a motor inn.

"You do not know?" she asked. "The king—Pelé."

"Oh," said Clive Toye. "I know."

Toye knew about Pelé, all right. He knew him like Ahab knew Moby Dick, having stalked the Brazilian over the past four years across two continents, through a 75,000-mile odyssey that he hoped would end here, in this motel outside of Brussels.

The first time Clive Toye ever saw Pelé was in 1958, in the World Cup tournament, in Stockholm, Sweden. Toye was a soccer writer for the Birmingham *Mail*. Pelé was the seventeen-year-old superstar of the Brazilian national team. "He was only seventeen, and he scored two goals in the final," Toye remembers. "I can still see every moment of one goal. He had his back to the goal and he caught the ball on his thigh, turned and shot it in. And I can still see this little kid, crying his eyes out with happiness when Brazil won the championship."

Over the years, as Toye grew into one of Britain's top sportswriters, he watched Pelé grow into the great-

CHAPTER EIGHT

est player soccer had ever known. Then, in 1971, he became general manager of the Cosmos. And, as much as he tried, he couldn't shake the crazy obsession that started to take hold of him: a vision of Pelé dressed in the Cosmos uniform. "That same year," Toye recalls, "I first talked to him casually about possibly playing for the Cosmos someday."

They met by a swimming pool at a hotel in Kingston, Jamaica, and talked under the shade of a hibiscus tree. "We talked about what him playing in the United States would do for soccer here, and what it would do for him," Toye says. "I told him that in one hundred years the photo on the wall of the man who did it for soccer in America should be his. I also reminded him that he had conquered the world, but that the single greatest market place is North America, and that he hadn't tapped that yet."

Pelé agreed—he would love to bring soccer to America, but not now. Certainly not now. Even considering it was out of the question. Toye changed the subject. He didn't push Pelé. All he had wanted to do was plant a seed.

"Then, at the World Cup last year, I got two hours with him," Toye says. "I had to be sneaked into his suite at the Intercontinental Hotel in Frankfurt at eight-thirty in the morning on one of his interview days. I told him of the progress of soccer in the United States, that the younger the players are, the better they are. I told him they knew of Pelé, but that they should have an opportunity to see Pelé play."

THE SIGNING OF PELÉ

But by then, Pelé had already decided to retire from soccer completely. The challenge was a tempting one —but no, again it was out of the question.

Like many star athletes, however, once Pelé was away from soccer, he missed it more than he had ever thought he would. He could have played anywhere in the world, but once he decided that he wanted to end his retirement, his messianic urge took over. At a meeting in Rome, he accepted the Cosmos' long-standing offer. Then, almost before Clive Toye had time to celebrate by lighting up one of his favorite cigars, suddenly Pelé changed his mind. A week later, he told the Cosmos he wouldn't play for them.

This wasn't the first time Clive Toye had come very close to signing an international superstar. Earlier in 1975, he had almost gotten Georgie Best's signature on a Cosmos contract. Best was a talented and fiery Irishman, a brilliant goal-scorer whose dazzling exploits on the soccer field were almost as well publicized as his exploits off the field. His brazen love affairs, his barroom fights, his all-around flamboyance attracted more notice from the world-wide press than he could stand. When he quit his career, at his peak, Toye brought him to the United States for a celebrated press conference, and the Cosmos actually signed Best to a contract. Then, for some reason known only to himself, Best decided to spend the summer on the beach in Spain, instead of on the soccer field in New York. Toye had failed, but that near-miss gave him the courage to persevere in pursuit of bigger game—Pelé.

CHAPTER EIGHT

"More than one hundred people told me I didn't have a chance of getting Best on a plane," Toye recalls, "but I brought him here and he told the people he wanted to play for me."

Fortified by that near-miss, Toye wasn't going to settle for another one. As soon as he heard that Pelé had changed his mind, he booked a reservation on the first plane out for Brazil. "We talked at a beach resort in Guaruja, and then in his offices in Santos," Toye recalls, "where his executive suite is decorated in purple and white—the royal purple, I thought—with a patio outside where he serves Café Pelé, his own coffee. It developed that they wanted fourteen minor changes, such as cooperation in a Pelé Foundation later on, where his children would go to school here, we would pay for his apartment, a no-trade clause."

But it turned out that the real reason behind Pelé's sudden reluctance was his suspicion of the Cosmos' offer. Toye recalls, "Julio Mazzei, his friend and adviser, told me, 'We have a feeling that the Cosmos are really an amateur team, that Warner Communications does not really exist, that Rafael de la Sierra (the Warner vice-president) is an international crook, that all these offers aren't going to happen. We have nightmares about this.'"

Toye spent hours trying to convince Pelé that the Cosmos' offer was a legitimate one. Proof that he had succeeded in convincing Pelé and his counselors was that he was now in Brussels, at the G.B. Motor Inn, standing in the room with the bouquet of roses in it,

THE SIGNING OF PELÉ

talking, while friends and strangers drifted in and out, with Pelé himself, a half hour before he was due to catch a plane for Morrocco.

"I think it is possible I will play again," Pelé said. "I would like to hear your offer."

Toye quickly, and anxiously, laid out the details of Warner Communications' proposal. Pelé listened, his face an expressionless mask. Then he picked up a leaf of hotel stationery. "Pelé's last offer," he wrote at the top—followed by a list of conditions, including how much, the length of the contract, and how payments should be made. Then, he signed it—"Edson=Pelé."

Clive Toye took that piece of hotel stationery, folded it, slipped it into his briefcase, and walked out of the room.

He never once touched the floor.

"Those two lines that Pelé wrote," says Toye, "had to be translated into thirty pages of contracts. But that was the moment that I first thought we would get him. His signature is interesting," Toye adds. "Pelé is only his nickname, you know. His real name is Edson Arantes do Nascimento, and in recent years he has signed his name 'Edson equals Pelé,' so that people will know that Edson *is* Pelé."

To get Pelé's signature on those thirty pages of contracts, it took money, but perhaps a heavy dose of pressure from what newspapers usually refer to as "the highest level of government" helped some, too. United States Secretary of State Henry Kissinger was an avid soccer fan who had attended the World Cup tournament in West Germany in the summer of 1974. During the long negotiations with the Cosmos, Kissinger sent Pelé the following telegram:

"Should you decide to sign a contract, I am sure your stay in the United States will substantially contribute to closer ties between Brazil and the United States in the field of sports."

Kissinger's cable was soon followed by a communiqué from the Brazilian foreign minister, Antonio Azeredo da Silviera, who likewise urged Pelé to sign a pact with the Cosmos.

Now Pelé could rest a little easier. Kissinger and da Silviera were effectively—if, perhaps, inadvertently—telling him that Warner Communications was no fly-by-night operation.

Still, given Pelé's longtime distrust of politics and politicians, it was undoubtedly Clive Toye's smooth tongue and persuasive, if soft, sell which resulted in that historic signing.

For, of course, Pelé did sign. And he did play for the Cosmos. Strangely enough, though, if history remembers Clive Toye, he hopes it's for another of his achievements—less publicized, but ultimately more satisfying. "All I want to be remembered for two hundred years from now," says Toye, "is that I was the coach of the Heathcote Hornets, who scored twenty-seven goals and allowed two, in winning the championship."

The Heathcote Hornets are a team of fourth graders, in Scarsdale, New York, where Clive Toye lives.

9

The Selling of Pelé

AT THE EDGEWATER HOTEL, in Seattle, Pelé spent a free afternoon fishing from the balcony of his room, three stories above the harbor. The hotel manager had given him a fishing rod, and, for bait, a bucket of salmon filets. Almost immediately Pelé hooked a small sand shark, which he hauled, wriggling, up to the balcony. A teammate struck it on the head, using the base of a table lamp, and Pelé leaned out the window to try again. Moments later, he caught a larger shark, so large, in fact, that it snapped the line just as he raised it up to the balcony.

"Fishing I like very much," he said, able now to converse quite fluently in English. "And baseball.

CHAPTER NINE

When I was a little boy in Bauru, in Brazil, my father was a baseball coach as well as a soccer player. So maybe I should have played baseball?"

Both CBS and the Seattle Sounders were grateful that Pelé had chosen soccer instead. CBS, which televised the Saturday game, was again rewarded with high ratings. Seattle was rewarded with 18,000 sports fans marching through the turnstiles of its stadium. And, as an unexpected bonus, Seattle won the game, too, with a score of 2–0, holding Pelé to only one shot on goal. In fact, the Sounders' best defense against him was the playing surface of their stadium. It was the second time in his career that Pelé had ever played on artificial turf, and the first time in conditions of extreme heat. The substance confounded him the way no flesh-and-blood defender could.

"Soccer was made to be played on real grass fields," he explained after the game. "There is a great difference between how the ball runs on a real grass field, and how it travels on a field composed of artificial surface.

"There are certain passing plays in soccer," he explained, "when you feed the ball to a teammate who is running downfield. The play calls for the ball to slow down so the man can catch up to it. But on an artificial surface, the ball just keeps on rolling and goes out of bounds. A good example of this is the pass I tried early in the first half," he recalled. "The play was supposed to be a short lead-pass to Jorge Siega.

THE SELLING OF PELÉ

But Siega couldn't catch up to the ball, and the play was dead. On a real grass field, I would have been able to put backspin on the ball, but you can't backspin a ball and have it stop where you want it to on an artificial surface.

"I also find that it is very hard to make long solo runs on those types of surfaces, and it takes you longer to switch directions when you trap a ball," Pelé added.

Hours after the game, Pelé was still complaining that his feet felt like they were burning. "It was very hot out there and the heat was coming right up from the surface," he said. "This caused burns around my soles, and I was also very tired after the game, something I don't feel after a game on grass. I'm going to wear a reinforced tennis sneaker when I play on artificial turf from now on."

During the game, Pelé wasn't the only one burning. At one point, the referee got hot under the collar, but the catalyst was Pelé, and not the artificial turf. "I was explaining to the referee that I had pushed my man off the ball with my shoulder," he said, illustrating by pushing a reporter with his shoulder. "That is all right. I didn't use my hands, which is *not* all right. Still, the referee took out the yellow card and booked me."

"What did the referee say to you?"

"He said to be quiet," Pelé answered, grinning, "so I went back to play."

The defeat left the Cosmos with a record of six

CHAPTER NINE

wins, eight losses. It was their second defeat in a row, and, with the NASL play-offs approaching, the Cosmos weren't even at the top of their division.

Next it was on to Vancouver, British Columbia, for the Cosmos' third game in five days. A record 26,495 showed up for the match against the Whitecaps, to watch the legendary Pelé lead the Cosmos to a victory that didn't count in the league standings. The field had an artificial surface, but it was cooler here in Vancouver, and Pelé, wearing tennis shoes he had borrowed from the Seattle team, seemed much more in control than he had the day before in Seattle. In the 2–1 victory, Pelé set up one goal with a perfect pass, and began to mesh again with his teammates. Afterwards, as was becoming a habit, Pelé added the defender charged with guarding him to his fan club.

"Some of our players were telling me before the game that since this was only an exhibition, Pelé wouldn't go out there killing himself," said the Whitecaps' Lee Wilson. "After the game, I told them that anytime they want the assignment of guarding him, they're welcome to it.

"I was faked out many, many times," he added. "When I backed off him, expecting him to try and dribble, he would put a loft-pass right over my head onto the feet of one of his teammates. Then, when I'd try and get real close to him, he'd back off the ball to get a running start, and then take off.

"I've never seen a man read the game so well in my life," Wilson continued. "He knows where every man on his team is at every time. I think the Cosmos missed too many passes that he sent to them, but the way he started both of his team's goals was really something. After the game," Wilson added, "he came over to me and told me that I played a pretty good game. I'm glad he told me so, because I think he made me look like a fool in so many different ways."

Each time Pelé received a pass from a teammate, the fans all leaped to their feet in anticipation.

"I would hear the fans yelling, and then try to brace myself for a fancy move by him," said Wilson. "Then he seemed to sense that I was expecting him to try something fancy, and he'd just get off a basic pass, and the Cosmos would be on the move."

After the game, Pelé was mobbed by a couple of hundred admirers. But with the help of Cosmos security men and Whitecaps players, Pelé—still waving to the crowd—was led to the dressing room. "It was a good game," Pelé said, trying to catch his breath. "It was very open and clean. Although this field isn't grass," he added, "it was a lot better to play on than the one we had in Seattle. At least we were able to work on some good passing plays, and that is what we will be doing, hopefully, on other non-grass fields. But don't get me wrong—I still don't like these types of surfaces."

That night, one of the Whitecaps' owners threw a cocktail party for Pelé and his teammates. For a while, Pelé stood socializing with the guests by the swimming pool, talking business and politics and money.

CHAPTER NINE

Then, suddenly, he noticed a group of Whitecaps players huddled alone on the far side of the pool. Pelé's face lit up, and that was the last the other guests saw of him. For the next two hours, he talked soccer with the rival players, recalling the time he played against one of them in Scotland, and giving them advice.

The next day the Cosmos flew home for a crucial game against Boston, at Randall's Island, on July 9. In attendance was a man who more and more was looming larger and larger in the entourage surrounding Pelé. His name was Dick Alford. Clive Toye had the task of signing Pelé. Julio Mazzei had the task of counseling and curing Pelé. Dick Alford's chore was less romantic, but no less crucial. He had the task of selling Pelé.

Alford had impressive credentials. He had spent eight years learning how to sell professional athletes from the greatest flesh-peddler of them all—agent Mark McCormack, who had made, among others, Arnold Palmer one of the richest athletes ever.

"Arnold Palmer had the best selling power of anyone in the United States," Alford said, "but Pelé out-universalizes Palmer. They don't know Arnold in Mozambique. At least they don't know him well enough to buy his pajamas."

To capitalize on Pelé's ability to reach the natives in some of the world's more remote outposts, plans to manufacture Pelé pajamas (with Astroturf soled-

THE SELLING OF PELÉ

feet as an option) were already being put into operation. The pajamas would fit nicely with the rest of the wardrobe Pelé had endorsed and Alford was ready to market: A Pelé knit shirt, a Pelé leather jacket, a Pelé denim leisure suit, Pelé knee socks, a Pelé rain hat, and even a pair of Pelé boxer shorts.

"My original projection was that we'd recoup the money we're paying Pelé in three years," said Clive Toye. "But now I'd be disappointed if it took us longer than two." Toye calculated that the Cosmos would earn $2.5 million as a result of signing Pelé.

"The possibilities are endless," Dick Alford added. "As far as marketing value, no sports figure except maybe Muhammad Ali can approach Pelé."

But the income from pajamas and underwear was penny ante compared to the staggering sums Alford hoped for from commercial tie-ins with airlines and automobiles and hotels. Alford was already negotiating with a major airline to use Pelé's name. Five or six automobile companies were competing for the honor of putting Pelé behind the wheel of their car. Kodak wanted to put his photograph in their ads. American Express wanted him to pay his dinner tabs with their credit card. And half a dozen international hotel chains were urging him to try out their water beds. "We're very conscious of the danger of overexposure," said Alford. "We'd rather make arrangements with eight or nine major companies than tie him to a hundred contracts that cheapen his image."

For their part, the Cosmos were planning to offer

an in-flight "Pelé Highlights" film, a catalogue of Pelé gift items, a 1978 World Cup Pelé tour package, and a Pelé booklet entitled *Places to Go in South America*, sort of a travel guide for people like Pelé—multimillionaires.

But mainly, the Cosmos—and the Warner executives who ran the franchise—were concentrating on keeping Pelé's image pure.

"The other day, someone sent me a movie script for Pelé," said Arnold Lewis, vice-president of a division of Warners called the Licensing Corporation of America (LCA), that would market the traditional sports items such as balls, sneakers, and so forth. "Apparently it called for him to show more than his feet. I sent it back and said no thanks."

By the time the Cosmos returned from the West Coast to New York to entertain the division-leading Boston Minutemen, they had boosted their office staff from seven to twenty, to handle the rush of season-ticket sales. Meanwhile, city agencies and the Cosmos' management were huddling to develop a plan to prevent another traffic jam on and around Randall's Island. At the Toronto game, for example, several thousand fans had to be turned away from the stadium. Traffic outside the stadium was so heavy that midway through the first half, Cosmos officials announced that 5,000 cars had been turned back from the ramp leading to the island.

After hearing that last claim, however, one New York writer felt compelled to go on record as a skeptic. The New York *Post*'s Larry Merchant—one of the most astute columnists anywhere—pointed out that the claims might be open to bias. The men who did the counting were attendants of the Kinney Parking System.

Kinney, of course, was a Warner Communications subsidiary.

"When they talk sports, it's always soccer," reported Miami Dolphins' head coach Don Shula, after visiting the rural Hungarian village where his father was born. "The only thing they know is that Pelé is playing for the New York Cosmos."

While Pelé was giving North American soccer legitimacy abroad, he was also making converts of those home-bred natives who hadn't believed that the man would measure up to his myth. Shep Messing, goalie for the Boston Minutemen, was a curly-headed free spirit—the only NASL player ever to be the centerfold, in the nude, of *Viva* magazine. A Harvard graduate, Messing had played two frustrating years with the Cosmos, with whom he had proved he had a tongue as agile as his body. He had Derek Sanderson's hair, Mark Spitz's face, and Muhammad Ali's mouth, but his mind was his own. At the 1970 Olympics, he was the United States team's starting goalie—up until opening-day ceremonies.

"The Olympic coach had decided the soccer team wasn't going to march in the parade. The coach thought that was the ultimate doomsday psych move,"

Shep says, grinning. "The competition would start shivering when they saw we weren't marching, that we were saving our legs for the games. I told him: 'Coach, I have trained four years to get here, and I am going to march in that parade.' "

Shep did, alone. That ended his Olympic soccer career. And as a Cosmo, Shep kept on marching solo.

"We were returning from our Mexican tour a couple of months ago," one player recalled in 1973, "traveling first class on the airplane. Suddenly coach Bradley noticed that passengers were whispering to each other, staring at some player sitting up front, then crinkling up their noses in disgust. Gordon peered around the seat in front of him—and his face got white. See, there was this *foot*, this *naked* foot, sticking out into the aisle. *Shep's* naked foot, *Shep* sitting with his bare feet in the aisle and his shirt unbuttoned to the waist."

It wasn't long before Messing became an ex-Cosmo. But he was still as brash as ever. The first time the Pelé-led Cosmos were to meet his Minutemen, before that disastrous game in which Pelé had almost been seriously mauled, Messing had trumpeted: "All I hear is Pelé, Pelé. All I read is Pelé, Pelé. The way I feel about this game is that Pelé has got to beat Shep Messing. Maybe it's because I grew up in New York," he added, "but to me he's just another player on the field. I'm just as worried about Liveric and Kerr as I am about him. Maybe if I was playing against Mickey Mantle or Willie Mays my knees would shake, but not against Pelé. When Pelé comes in on me tonight," Messing had concluded, "I'm not going to stand there applauding. I'm going to come charging out like a wild man, just like I always do."

Once that night, Messing did come charging out like a wild man—to shield the fallen Pelé from the over-zealous fans who were threatening to dismember him.

Before tonight's game, the first thing Pelé did when he stepped onto the field was walk over to Messing, and thank him for reacting so quickly in his defense in Boston. It was soon evident that Messing had lost his skepticism about Pelé. "He's not only a great guy, he's a great competitor," Messing said. "Once, in that first game, when he came in on me, I tapped him in his belly, and he got a little angry. So the next time we came up against one another, he made sure he gave me a push in the gut. And then, late in the first half," he added, "we tripped over one another. When he saw I had the ball, he patted me on the head and said, 'Okay, Okay.'"

Pelé not only won Messing over before that match at Downing Stadium, he beat him badly during the match. With about twenty minutes gone in the second half, and the Cosmos already leading, 3–0, Pelé demonstrated exactly how the man became the myth. He took a pass from midfielder Johnny Kerr, faked two men out of position, then fed the ball right back to Kerr, who stunned Messing with a fifteen-yarder.

"When Pelé got the ball on that play," Messing

said later, "I thought he was going to let loose. Once he switched the play, and fed the ball back to Kerr, I had no chance to stop the ball."

"It's on plays like this where Pelé really excels," explained Julio Mazzei. "Everyone thinks he's going to shoot, and he fools them with a swift return pass, and the goalie is out of position."

Pelé didn't score a single goal; yet, according to coach Gordon Bradley, he had "played one of the best games he's played in the past year and a half."

The Cosmos had won, 3–1, before 18,126 spectators. They were now 7–8 for the season, and back in first place in the NASL's Northern Division.

10

Planting the Seed

THE COSMOS' euphoria at being in first place soon evaporated. "If we are to make the play-offs," said Gordon Bradley, on the eve of a game at Downing Stadium against the Portland Timber, "we'll have to win almost all of the four games we have left to play at home, as well as some of the key road games, like the one next Saturday night in Toronto."

But the Timber beat the Cosmos convincingly, 2–1. The Cosmos slipped into a second-place tie. And even worse than the setback in the league standings was the setback to their morale. "This was the poorest game we've played since I joined the team," said Pelé. "We did everything wrong."

CHAPTER TEN

Both Pelé and goalie Sam Nusam had contributed strong efforts. Their teammates had contributed little more than wild passes and futile tackles, scrambling helter-skelter around the field like a gaggle of Keystone Cops. "We made errors that a professional team has no right to make," Pelé complained. "But," he added, "at least we can't play that badly again."

Pelé was mistaken. Three days later, the Cosmos lost their second game in a week, 3–0. The defeat by Toronto, the divisional leaders, dropped the Cosmos into third place in the Northern Division. But even more worrisome than the defeat was the injury inflicted on Pelé by a Toronto defender. Early in the second half, Pelé took the ball, dribbled past one defender, then another. Just as he was going to sprint past a third, someone brought him down with a vicious kick to his left thigh.

He stayed in the game, but it was obvious he was in pain. As soon as the game ended, Julio Mazzei led him into the dressing room and assessed the damage. Then he turned to Gordon Bradley and Clive Toye. It would be impossible, he informed them, for Pelé to play in the Cosmos' upcoming exhibition match in St. Louis.

"We were losing," said Gordon Bradley, explaining why he hadn't taken Pelé out of the game as soon as he saw him start to hobble, "and since Pelé likes to lose less than anyone else, he made his own decision to stay in the game. In fact, though," Bradley admitted, "he hasn't been one hundred percent fit for some time now. But you know what a great athlete he is. He plays hurt and you don't even know it."

Everyone would soon learn what it meant to the Cosmos' profits when Pelé was so hurt he couldn't play at all. "We got on the phone to St. Louis, and told them that although we were still ready to play the game, Pelé wouldn't play since he had a strain and a bruise above his left thigh," Gordon Bradley reported. "We gave them the option of either having the game played without Pelé, or scheduling it for another time. They called back and told us that since many of the ten thousand seats were sold because of Pelé, they'd rather postpone the game, and we agreed."

Meanwhile, Toronto had gained more than a simple victory. A sellout crowd had turned out to see Pelé— a crowd so enthusiastic, that, after the game, they knocked Pelé's bodyguard, Pedro Garay, to the ground in a wild scramble to get the Brazilian star's autograph. According to a Toronto spokesman, the size of the crowd and the pitch of their enthusiasm had probably saved that ailing franchise from going out of business.

Pelé had only three days' rest before the Cosmos met San Jose at Downing Stadium. Despite the fact that he was still in pain, he decided to play. The Cosmos had only five regular season games left, and they had to beat San Jose to keep alive their play-off hopes. It took them a fifteen-minute overtime period to resolve the game in their favor, but the Cosmos did manage to eke out a 2-1 win.

Afterwards, in the Cosmos dressing room, Pelé

CHAPTER TEN

stretched out on a bench, the sweat dripping off his body, as Julio Mazzei pressed ice packs to both of his thighs.

The Cosmos' next game was an exhibition against Dallas at Texas Stadium, before a crowd of 26,127. Over the past few weeks, the Cosmos had been adding hordes of new players to their roster—from Brazil, from other NASL clubs—trying to bolster their defense and to give Pelé help on offense. But today, for seventy-two minutes, Pelé didn't need anybody's help. He was at his best, easily avoiding the tackles of defenders, giving his teammates sharp and productive passes, outleaping taller defenders. Then, suddenly, Pelé was on the ground, clutching his left thigh. Two minutes later, he limped off the field, and the Cosmos were beaten, 3–2.

A few days later, doctors announced that Pelé had suffered a torn hamstring muscle. He wouldn't be able to play at all in the Cosmos match against Rochester.

The day of that game, July 30, as Pelé emerged from his chauffeur-driven limousine outside the players' entrance to Downing Stadium, a group of about thirty kids ran up to him, and asked him for his autograph. "I'll sign for you," Pelé said, dressed colorfully in a white jacket, blue pants and a multihued shirt, "but I'm sorry that I cannot play tonight. You come next week and you will see me play."

The incident was typical. No matter what his personal problems at the moment, Pelé has never inflicted

PLANTING THE SEED

them on his fans. "I appreciate the crowds around me," he once said. "Especially the kids. I know that when I was growing up, soccer was one of the few things I could enjoy. Seeing a top player was always a big thrill. Now I get a thrill myself by having the kids around me. Of course," he added, "sometimes the people can get *too* enthusiastic."

One morning, at Caracas airport, in Venezuela, Pelé and his teammates were trapped in their plane for four hours, until police finally managed to clear the field of riotously enthusiastic fans. In Dakar, Senegal, he barely escaped with his life, when, at four in the morning, a mob tried to pull their hero off the bus that was taking him from his plane to the airport waiting room. In Milan, a crowd surrounded him for hours, while he hid behind a large pillar, waiting for a chance to sprint to a car. In the Ivory Coast, 15,000 fans lined both sides of the road leading from the airport to the city of Abidjan, shouting "Pelé, Pelé," as their idol moved past in a convertible car. "It was like a parade," Julio Mazzei recalls, "for a president."

Sometimes, however, it was difficult for Pelé to reconcile all this adulation with the need to be a team player. Sometimes the two roles conflicted. When, for example, Queen Elizabeth invited him to a special audience during the 1966 World Cup tournament in England, Pelé the superstar wanted very much to accept. But the Brazilian national team was in "concentration"—the monastic ritual Brazilians practice before each game. The Brazilian coach, Vicente Feola, didn't think it was right for one player to leave those spartan surroundings while everyone else had to stay, but he left the final decision up to Pelé. Pelé the team player graciously, but firmly, refused the Queen's invitation. And that refusal created an uproar among the English press. Pelé had already acquired the reputation for being a moody loner—the by-product of his need to surround himself with bodyguards to get any privacy at all, and to keep his romance with Rosie a secret, thereby inducing the world into thinking he had no private life at all. In fact, he was portrayed in the London *Sunday Times* as a "sad millionaire . . . an introverted, remote figure imprisoned in the shell that protects him from the crushing weight of his fame."

"That's not true at all," Pelé replied sharply. "In refusing the Queen, I was doing what the team wanted. I would never do something like that out of temperament. On the contrary, I feel that, in my position, I have a special responsibility *not* to be temperamental."

But most of all, Pelé has been careful how he influences the fans who adulate him most—the kids. He neither drinks nor smokes, and he will not endorse tobacco or liquor. Even when his teammates were toasting their 1962 victory in the World Cup final, Pelé would only sip water.

Thanks to Tommy Ord, a clever goal-scorer just purchased from Rochester, the Cosmos beat the Lancers without Pelé, and that 2–0 victory kept their play-off hopes glimmering—if ever so dimly. But the game lacked the excitement Pelé would have injected.

PLANTING THE SEED

And it lacked something else, too—a capacity crowd. The attendance of little more than 8,000 was more than in pre-Pelé days, but half what the Cosmos had been drawing since the Brazilian arrived. Even Pelé couldn't help noticing, from his seat on the Cosmos' bench. "Where," he asked, "are all the people?"

It was a question that was being asked more and more around the Cosmos' headquarters, too. Attendance had dropped noticeably since Pelé had joined the team six weeks before. In his first game with the Cosmos, the exhibition against Dallas, 21,278 fans had turned out to welcome him. A few days later, when Pelé made his official league debut, the number of spectators swelled to 22,500, and the Cosmos were forced to turn away a few thousand more.

But lately, attendance had begun to decline. Two weeks before, against Portland, the Cosmos had drawn only 13,421; a week ago, against San Jose, attendance dropped to 11,127. And now, against Rochester, a meager 8,000.

"I think the trouble is in Downing Stadium," said Clive Toye. "Months before Pelé came here, I said if we got Pelé we hoped to average 12,000. I was incredibly overwhelmed that 22,500 showed up for the second game, after the fiasco we had with Pelé's debut. Quite honestly, we weren't prepared to handle that many people. The parking, the police, the security, the ushers—all were understaffed. We've got thousands of letters from fans who said they attended the first two Pelé games, but wouldn't come back."

CHAPTER TEN

But there were other factors apart from the condition of the stadium and the Cosmos' own unpreparedness. "The weather," Toye argued. "People don't want to take the chance of sitting in an open stadium and getting soaking wet or struck by lightning," he added, referring to the fact that New York had had its wettest summer in decades.

And last, but certainly far from least important, there was the product. "We haven't been winning," Toye finally admitted. "And nobody likes to watch a loser, Pelé or no Pelé."

New York sportswriters had also begun to adopt a less idolatrous tone, not only toward the Cosmos, but toward Pelé himself. Dick Young of the *Daily News* ran this item in his column of July 31, after Pelé's injury.

"Again. That makes twice within the last two weeks. Same leg. Same thigh pull. Each time the projected absence grows longer. Each time promoters on the Cosmo schedule shudder.

"Pelé is no goof-off, no joker. If anything, he forces himself back into action prematurely, fully aware of the fact that people have bought tickets around the country in expectation of seeing him, him alone. It is not immodest to be aware of this. He feels terrible about it. He didn't expect it to happen, this disability.

"Why not? Many of us did. I remember the big press conference at the 21 Club last month, the mob scene that attended his formal signing. He was thirty-four now, he had laid out almost two years.

" 'How do you expect to escape leg injuries, muscle pulls?' he was asked by realistic newsmen.

" 'When you keep your body in shape, as I have all my life,' said Pelé, 'thirty-four is young. I do not think I have to worry about such things.'

"To be President of the United States, thirty-four is young, too young. To be a professional athlete, thirty-four is not young. It is old. If Pelé wonders why these things have never happened to him before, the answer is simple. He was never thirty-four before."

Even without Pelé, the Cosmos were favored to defeat the hapless Hartford Bicentennials, who, while compiling a record of four wins against fourteen losses, had proved themselves masters of ineptitude. But the Cosmos managed to buck the oddsmakers, losing to Hartford, 3–1, in what was undoubtedly their poorest game of the season—that is, their poorest game until their *next* game, against the Boston Minutemen. In a contest they had to win in order to keep even the slimmest of play-off hopes alive, the Cosmos simply collapsed, displaying little talent in that 5–0 loss, and even less heart. So displeased was the small crowd of 4,445 at Boston's Nickerson Field, they actually laughed aloud at some of the Cosmos' more futile moves, especially when the newly acquired fullback from Brazil, De, would seem to tire after running six or seven yards; when Alfredo Lamas would pass the ball to a Boston player instead of a teammate; when Julio Correa would fall to the turf without anyone touching him, then look pleadingly at the referee, as if he had been fouled; and when another Brazilian, Manoel Maria, kept sending the ball across the field—seven out of ten times—to the opponents.

"From the start of the game we didn't look good," said Pelé, still on the bench, as he greeted Boston's pair of Portuguese stars, Eusebio and Simoes, after the game. "We got worse as the game went on, and Boston got better. We played with no heart, no drive, and little skill," he added. "If Boston had wanted to, they could have beaten us, 8–0."

The Cosmos defeated the Minutemen in a return match at Downing Stadium—again without Pelé—the following Wednesday, but the victory came too late. The Cosmos had been eliminated from the playoffs, and Pelé's first season, which began with such promise, had ended in disappointment.

To recoup some of that money they had invested in Pelé, the Cosmos traveled all over the country to play, during the month of September, fifteen exhibition games, then embarked on a international tour that would take them to Sweden, Turkey, Norway, Italy, and Haiti. By the time the Cosmos reached Europe, Pelé had recovered completely, and thrilled full houses across the continent with his goal-scoring magic. Only the Italian team Roma was able to prevent him from scoring, despite the fact that everywhere he played he was usually triple-teamed.

But the fact that he could still wow them in Oslo and Stockholm and Rome had never been in doubt. What *was* in doubt was whether, in Pelé's *second* season with the Cosmos, leading them from the start, Pelé could help the NASL leap forward to true big-league status.

Naturally, though, Pelé didn't have any doubts at all. "The seed will be in the ground, whatever happens," said Pelé, sitting in his limousine with Rosie beside him. "The seed could be a big tree; it depends on the treatment given to the little seed."

Then he gently laid his head on his wife's shoulder and drifted off to sleep.

Don Kowet

Don Kowet is the former managing editor of *Sport* magazine and the author of *Vida Blue* and *Golden Toes*.

WHITEFIELD PUBLIC LIBRARY
WHITEFIELD, N.H. 03598

DATE DUE

JUL 31 1976		
MAY 2 1978		
MAY 18 1978		
OCT. 7 1978		
SEP. 5 1981		
NOV. 7 1981		
FEB. 4 1982		
AUG. 13 1987		
OCT. 14 1989		
JUL 2 1994		

J 796.33 Kowet

DISCARDED